POEMS OF NANCY CUNARD

POEMS OF NANCY CUNARD

From the Bodleian Library

Edited with an Introduction by John Lucas

TRENT EDITIONS

Published by Trent Editions, 2005

Trent Editions
School of Arts, Communication and Culture
Nottingham Trent University
Clifton Lane
Nottingham NG11 8NS

http://human.ntu.ac.uk/research/trenteditions/mission.html

Typeset by Roger Booth Associates, Hassocks, West Sussex BN6 8AR
Printed by Antony Rowe Limited, Bumper's Farm Industrial Estate,
Chippenham, Wiltshire SN14 6LH

ISBN 1-84233-107-8

Contents

Acknowledgements

The editor wishes first and foremost to thank Dorothy Thompson, who gave permission to make use of Nancy Cunard's poems now housed in the Bodleian as part of the Thompson family papers. Without this permission this edition could not have been undertaken. Thanks are also due to Joseph Pridmore for penetrating the arcanum of the Bodleian in order to photocopy the poems, to Frances Banks for rendering the photocopies into legible typescript, and to Sam Ward for his painstaking labours in copy editing and in tracking down even the most elusive of references and allusions.

Introduction

Sometime in pre-war 1914, Lady Diana Cooper paid a visit to the studio flat near Bloomsbury which the eighteen year-old Nancy Cunard shared with Iris Tree. The place looked a tip, and the visitor made some remark that implicitly linked the flat's squalid appearance with Lady Cunard's concern about her daughter's behaviour. But Nancy would have none of it. 'My mother's having an affair with Thomas Beecham,' she told her visitor, 'I can do as I like.'

At that period of her life, Nancy Cunard's likes were similar to those of most young women of her class: a whirl of dances, parties, and the company of what her biographer, Anne Chisholm, calls 'the more unusual young men.' Among these were Evan Morgan, son and heir of Lord Tredegar, Edward Wyndham Tennant, son of Lord Glenconner and nephew of Margot Asquith, who rejoiced under the nickname of 'Bimbo' and saw himself as a poet in the making, the young Chilean painter, poet and amateur boxer, Alvaro Guevara, Osbert and Sacheverell Sitwell, and raffish, not to say *louche* figures from the world of Bohemia, including Wyndham Lewis and Ezra Pound. Because Nancy was beautiful, tall and slim, with a distinctive voice and way of speaking—'gracefully turbulent, arrogantly disruptive, brave', so Iris Tree recalled—most of the men fell in love with her, though she did not love them.

But with the outbreak of hostilities, Nancy changed at least some of her ways. Whether she saw marrying as her contribution to the war effort isn't clear, but she certainly chose a warrior for her husband. Born in Australia, Sydney Fairbairn had grown up in an English country house, was wealthy, athletic, good-looking, and entirely conventional. After being wounded at Gallipoli, he was evacuated to Cairo, then sent home on leave. The following year he and Nancy became engaged. The fact that Lady Cunard seems to have tried to dissuade Nancy from marrying Fairbairn no doubt strengthened her daughter's determination to go ahead. For Nancy Cunard was very much part of that emerging revolution of the young against the old. As far as she was concerned, Lady Cunard's discretion about her love affair with Beecham was mere hypocrisy. And while she had found life with her father, Sir Bache Cunard, at Nevill Holt, the family house in rural Leicestershire where forty servants were regularly employed, increasingly dull, neither did she want to be beholden to her American mother, born Maud Burke in California in 1872, whom Sir Bache had met when the young girl—half his age—visited

London in 1894. As an heiress, Nancy could afford to do as she liked. And so in November 1916, she and Fairbairn were married. Among the guests were Lady Diana Manners, who would later play the part of Britannia, stoned, at a post-war pageant held at the Albert Hall on 27 November 1918, Lady Randolph Churchill, the writer George Moore (an old friend of her father's who was fond of Nancy), the newly knighted Beecham, and Ivor Novello. Chisholm notes that one newspaper used the occasion of the wedding to announce that Nancy Cunard 'will be one of the leaders of society after the war.' At the time that must have seemed a reasonable enough prediction.

In the same month as the Cunard-Fairbairn marriage took place the first of six anthologies of new verse appeared. The series, edited by the Sitwells and called *Wheels*, took its name from the title poem of the initial anthology, and its author, as with six other poems in that first publication, was Nancy Cunard.

> I sometimes think that all our thoughts are wheels
> Rolling forever through the painted world,
> Moved by the cunning of a thousand clowns
> Dressed paper-wise, with blatant rounded masks …

There is not much point is directing critical fire power at these frail lines. Enough to note that their would-be scepticism, the sense of society whose behaviour is mechanistic, undifferentiated, does at least hint at dissatisfactions that as yet Cunard has no way of focusing. And there seems no reason to doubt the genuineness of her feeling that something is amiss in the 'painted world.' But what exactly? Is her angst merely that *ersatz* distress of the poor little rich girl or might it have a deeper cause? I don't think it is possible to try to provide answers to these questions. What is certain is that from now on Cunard wanted to be taken seriously as a poet and that she wouldn't be content with turning out *vers de société*. She also wanted to be a free spirit. Poor Fairbairn had therefore to go. Their divorce was not completed until 1925, but well before that Nancy Cunard's increasingly bohemian ways had ruled out continuation of marriage to a man who simply wanted a life of placid normality.

In June 1920, Cunard recorded in her diary her belief that she suffered from 'a shocking super sensitiveness. Oh how often have I cursed that, and now more than ever—it stands in the way of everything, distorts my life and makes me almost impossible to live, get on with I should say. Hidden, it's even worse, this gnawing and probing and exaggerating and lacerating state of mind. I seem to want too much, hence a mountain of unhappiness.' Mere self-indulgence? Perhaps, but a few months later she notes: 'How hidden and remote one is from the obscure vortex of England's revolutionary troubles, coal strikes, etc. So much newspaper talk does it seem to me, and yet—is it going to be always so?'[1] Put these two entries back to back and it isn't wildly speculative to suppose that Nancy Cunard's way of resolving the unhappiness she felt at what was still an essentially frivolous life lay in committing herself to the 'hidden and remote'. Besides, there's a stir of excitement in the words 'revolutionary troubles'.

Some eighty years later that phrase can look merely hysterical. But this was not how matters seemed in 1920, a year of widespread and justified anxieties about England's future. The generation to which Cunard belonged, including the Bright Young Things with whom she is sometimes misleadingly identified, shared a gloom-ridden awareness that the recent war to end all wars had in fact made future wars inevitable. The 1917 revolution in Russia awoke hopes or fears—depending which side you took—for revolution elsewhere. And the 1920s was a time for taking sides. The hooded hordes that are glimpsed in *The Waste Land* (1921) swarming over endless plains might even be massing in England itself. In the spring of 1920 dockers refused to load arms onto ships bound for Poland, where they were intended for eventual use against the Red Army. In October the miners went on strike. That same month, what became dubbed 'the Battle of Downing Street' took place. In the words of the *Daily Mirror*'s reporter, 'wild scenes were witnessed in Whitehall and Downing Street … during a demonstration by 10,000 unemployed, headed by the mayors of fifteen London boroughs where there is a Labour majority. Baton charges were frequent, and at one point mounted police cleared Whitehall at a gallop.'[2] In his great poem 'Nineteen Nineteen', W. B. Yeats had wondered, forebodingly, 'And what rough beast, its hour come round at last,/Slouches towards Bethlehem to be born.' Rough beasts might slouch, the working class male, at least in the eyes of his betters, certainly did. Hooded hordes and wild beasts: Demos on the prowl. In 1920 the Communist Party of Great Britain came into existence.

Unlike the mass membership of the Labour Party, however, the numbers of those joining the CPGB in its early years were more or less invisible to the naked eye and didn't include Nancy Cunard. For all her doubts and shudders of distaste at the social whirl, she was for the moment still involved in the kinds of activities certain to find their way into gossip columns. In the spring of 1920 she was introduced to Michael Arlem who, in common with just about every man she ever met, fell in love with her and then drew on her for the heroine of his 1922 novel, *Piracy*, although by the time the novel appeared she was pursuing an affair with Aldous Huxley. Huxley duly introduced a fictional version of her into *Antic Hay* (1924), by which time she was more often in Paris than in London. She was also working with renewed energy at her poetry. It is a measure of how seriously she took her writing that she wasn't afraid to send a new poem to Ezra Pound, who wasn't afraid to tell her what he thought of it. 'Why, why the devil do you write in that obsolete dialect and with the cadences of the late Alfred Tennyson… And it is damned hard to get the order of words in a poem as simple and natural as that of speech. Iambic pentameter is a snare because it constantly lets one in for dead phrases like 'in this midnight hour' … Twice 'all, *all* friendly, *all* gay … One must get the palate clean, must get the speech of poetry even more vivid than that of prose … Damn it all, midnight is midnight, it is not "this midnight hour", also you twist the tenses for the sake of rhyme. And lots, lots of words that do not add anything to the presentation, but tell the reader nothing he wouldn't know if you had left them out…'[3] It says much for Cunard's readiness to take a full look at the worst of her writing that she kept this unsparing letter.

It and the poem it savages belong to 1921, the year in which Cunard's first collection appeared. *Outlaws* was published in London by Elkin Matthews and Marrot, a small but distinguished firm that had published several of the luminaries of the 1890s and had also seen into print early work by both Eliot and Pound. The fact that *Outlaws* was subsidised by the poet herself shouldn't therefore be taken to imply that this was Vanity Press work, and reviews were on the whole complimentary, even enthusiastic. But Edgell Rickword, noting the book in the *New Statesman*, was more cautious. 'One feels the pulse of an original mind beating through a rather uncongenial medium.'[4] This is tactful. Cunard did have an original mind, although this could be no more than glimpsed through verse which was for the most part inept where not downright bad.

> Love has destroyed my life, and all too long
> Have I been enemy with life, too late
> Unlocked the secrets of existence! there
> Found but the ashes of a fallen city
> Stamped underfoot … ('The Wreath')

'And give up verse, my girl', you almost hear the voice of Pound's Mr Nixon whispering.

Instead, two years later, Cunard brought out another collection, called *Sublunary*. By now poems of hers had appeared in such places as the *Nation* and the *Observer*, and she must have been buoyed up by words of encouragement from her old friend, George Moore, who urged her to work at her craft. 'This is well enough for a first book,' he wrote, after he had read *Outlaws*, 'but ultimate genius is not in explosions but in restraints.' *Sublunary* was published by Hodder and Stoughton in June 1923, and unfortunately doesn't suggest that she had gained much from Moore's advice. The new poems were characterised by the same vapidity and slack rhythms that had marred *Outlaws*. And although *Sublunary* was on the whole well or at least tolerantly reviewed, it doesn't mark an advance on its predecessor.

If Cunard sensed this, she wasn't ready to give up. Another two years, another new book, this time published by the Woolfs' Hogarth Press. A long poem, *Parallax* has, as Anne Chisholm rightly says, 'powerful, sometimes obtrusive, links with T.S. Eliot's *The Waste Land*, which had obviously had a profound effect on Nancy when it was published in 1922.' Chisholm quotes Raymond Mortimer's praise for the poem's 'desolate sort of beauty'. The writer is one, he claims, 'who perseveres through a life whose point he (sic) continually seeks in vain, too intelligent either to be content with one or to accept the facile explanations that soothe others.'[5]

What neither Mortimer nor the poet herself could know was that in a cancelled passage of *The Waste Land* Eliot had produced a savage caricature of a certain 'Fresca', a combination of upper-class whore—'A doorstep dunged by every dog in town'—and would-be writer, and that Fresca, in part at least, is almost certainly based on Nancy Cunard.

> The Scandinavians bemused her wits,
> The Russians thrilled her to hysteric fits.
> For such chaotic misch-masch potpourri
> What are we to expect but poetry?
> When restless nights distract her brain from sleep
> She may as well write poetry, as count sheep.
> And on those nights when Fresca lies alone,
> She scribbles verse of such a gloomy tone
> That cautious critics say, her style is quite her own.
> Not quite an adult, and still less a child,
> By fate misbred, by flattering friends beguiled,
> Fresca's arrived (the Muses Nine declare)
> To be a sort of can-can salonnière.[6]

In his biography of Eliot, Peter Ackroyd, who doesn't comment on the Fresca episode, suggests that Cunard was among several women who tried to lure the poet away from his wife, although his evidence for this assertion amounts to no more than hearsay.[7] Chisholm, who accepts the plausibility of the identification of Fresca with Cunard, remarks that the passage's bitterness 'might be explained by the contrast between the struggles of Eliot and his wife against illness and poverty, and the affluent, leisured existence of Nancy; not to mention the contrast between the difficulties he and Pound experienced in getting their work into print and appreciated and the ease with which the well-connected amateur, Nancy, found publishers and respectful reviewers for her work.'[8]

This is magnanimous. It also recognises a limitation in Cunard which by 1925 she was, I think, coming to recognise in herself and to labour to correct. While she could do nothing about being a well-connected amateur beyond making life difficult for her mother, she could try to do something to counter the implied charge of dilettantism which she must have felt others directed at her and which, more to the point, she must have thought was deserved. What direction or purpose, after all, did her life have? The honest answer is, precious little. Hence, perhaps, the moment in *Parallax* where Cunard enjoins herself to 'Think now how friends grow old' and wonders whether she is herself no more than 'a vagrant … most surely at the beginning yet.' Her existence was without doubt that of a high class vagrant: constant only in its inconstancy. For years she had moved restlessly between England and France, shuttled between town and country, had tried and discarded lovers as the mood took her.

II.

But the death of her father at the end of 1925 seems to have marked the end of her beginning. In the spring of 1926, back in Paris, Cunard began another love affair, this time more serious, committed; and although the affair itself lasted only two years, it was to have a profound affect on her. Louis Aragon was a key figure among the Surrealists, whose reputation was then at its peak, in Paris and beyond. Moreover, Aragon was a political radical—he joined the communist party at the beginning of 1927—and Cunard was quick to identify with both his artistic and political commitments. With money her father had left her, she bought a house in Normandy and in the early summer of 1928, having acquired a hand press, she and Aragon began to learn to handle type. Her house, Le Puits Carre, became the home of the Hours Press, which in the next few years was to produce work by, among others, Richard Aldington, Aragon himself, Roy Campbell, Robert Graves, George Moore, Ezra Pound, Laura Riding, as well as a poem by an unknown writer called

Samuel Beckett, *Whorescope*, which Cunard published in midsummer 1930 in a limited edition of 200 copies.

By the time Beckett's book appeared the affair with Aragon had ended and Cunard had started one which Chisholm calls the most crucial relationship in her life. In Venice in the autumn of 1928 she went to a hotel to dance to music that was provided by a black American jazz band, Eddie South and his Alabamians. Afterwards, the musicians were invited to join Cunard's party for drinks. There and then she appears to have fallen for the pianist, a man some ten years her senior called Henry Crowder. Although his musical commitments at first kept the couple apart, by the end of the year the band had broken up (someone, probably Sidney Bechet, had tried to shoot the banjoist), and Crowder moved in with Nancy and began to help her with her press.

There is no reason to doubt the genuineness of their affection for each other, though there were occasions when Crowder was for Cunard rather more a Cause than a person. Harold Acton remembered her imploring her lover to 'be more *African*.' 'But I *ain't* African. I'm *American*', Crowder not unreasonably replied. The most important fruit of their labours is the anthology, *Negro*, for which she undertook the major part of the work. So much so indeed that when the book was published in 1934 it was under her name, although she dedicated it to 'Henry Crowder, my first Negro friend.' By then, their relationship had come to an amicable close. Nevertheless, at the time of the book's appearance both were in London, Crowder living with a black girl friend, Cunard with Edgell Rickword, who as reader for Wishart & Co., had persuaded the firm to take on *Negro*. The fact that she was paying for publication of her massive work—it ran to no fewer than 855 pages— must have helped to ease the firm's decision. Wishart had therefore no great reason to regret the book's indifferent reception, nor the poor sales. (Several hundred copies of the 1,000 print run were still unsold when Hitler's bombers destroyed the stock.) She on the other hand was furious with what she saw as at best lackadaisical attempts to publicise a book at which she had laboured so devotedly. Her anger is understandable. For, whatever its flaws, *Negro* is a major achievement, and it is therefore good to know that when a shortened version was reprinted in New York in 1970, the book met with a far more sympathetic response than had greeted its initial appearance. Unfortunately this came too late for Nancy Cunard, who had died in 1965.

Negro is motivated by a generous radical politics. Although Cunard never became a paid-up member of the CPGB, by 1934 she was to all intents and purposes working for the Communist cause. In August 1935 she journeyed, alone, to Moscow. She also worked as a correspondent for the Chicago-based Associated Negro Press, a press Agency specialising in copy for black papers, and in this capacity she fulminated against Mussolini's annexing of Abyssinia. Then came Spain.

Soon after the so-called Civil War began in July 1936, Cunard paid her first ever visit to Spain, filing copy for her news agency, and meeting several writers and artists. Among them was the Chilean poet Pablo Neruda, who under the Republic was acting as his country's consul in Madrid, and whom she took with her to her French home where she at once set him to work at the press. Her plan was to produce a series of six leaflets called 'Les Poètes de Monde Défendent le Peuple Espagnol'. (Auden's great poem 'Spain' would appear in the fifth such leaflet.) She also laid plans for another publication. The idea was to invite as many writers as she could think of to state their position on the war. She would then print their answers, which she took for granted would be overwhelmingly in favour of the Republic, and which would therefore bolster the morale of those fighting for the Republican cause as well as reveal how widespread was intellectual disapproval of the official British policy of non-intervention. The questions 'Are you for, or against, the legal Government and the People of Republican Spain? Are you for, or against, Franco and Fascism?', were accordingly sent 'To the Writers and Poets of England, Scotland, Ireland and Wales'. The answers came in, and in November 1937 one of the most famous of all works to appear at that extraordinary time, *Authors Take Sides on the Spanish War*, was published as a sixpenny pamphlet. Of the 148 contributors, only sixteen were neutral (including Eliot, Pound and H. G. Wells) and a mere five, among them Edmund Blunden and Evelyn Waugh, took the side of Franco and the Falangists. The rest, from Lascelles Amercrombie to Leonard Woolf, proclaimed themselves with various degrees of enthusiasm on the side of the Spanish Republic.[9]

For all her commitment to and work for the Republican cause, Cunard still found time in 1938 to pay a visit to Tunisia with a friend of long-standing, the writer and exile from England, Norman Douglas. Then, with Franco triumphant, and the onset of war against Hitler, she left France in January 1940. Her destination was first Chile, where she met Neruda again and was introduced to his friends. After Chile came Mexico and finally the West Indies. Unable to return to occupied France, she settled for England, where she took lodgings in London and began work on several projects, chief among them perhaps an anthology by English writers in celebration of France. This was eventually published, in French, by La France Libre, in 1944, and included among its seventy contributors poets as different from each other as Sir John Squire and Hugh MacDiarmid. 1944 was the year in which a collection of her own poems should have appeared, although for reasons to be discussed later the publication never happened.

If this was a blow to her, it was far less heavy than the one awaiting her in France. With the liberation of Paris she was free to return to what she thought of as her adopted country. Almost at once she was on her way, and in June 1945 she published an exultant letter from Paris in *Horizon*, praising the renewed activity in 'all things of the intellect and of the arts.' Then she journeyed on to her home.

To her horror she discovered that Le Puits Carre had been wrecked and most of its contents plundered or smashed. The press, though rusty, had managed to escape the general destruction, but virtually all the correspondence relating to her work for it had been carried off: letters from Aldington, Aragon, Breton, Roy Campbell, Eliot, Ronald Firbank, Robert Graves, Aldous Huxley, Ezra Pound, Arthur Symons—all gone. Gone, too, was her collection of art works, gone the equally valuable collection of African primitive sculptures, gone the African ivory bracelets, gone her oriental rugs. But what made the horror almost unbearable was her realisation that all this had been done, not by the occupying Nazis, but by the locals, people she had thought of as her friends.

She took legal action. A case for compensation was made up and presented to the courts but in the end she got nothing. Chisholm says that she was 'convinced there were political motives behind the decision', and this may well have been so. It may also mark the beginning of what seems to have been an increasing paranoia that was to scar her remaining years. Moreover, heavy smoking and drinking were beginning to affect her health. And yet, astonishingly, these were also years of continued energetic work and writing, including two memoirs of older writers who had meant much to her. *Grand Man: Memories of Norman Douglas*, was published by Secker and Warburg in 1954, and two years later Rupert Hart-Davis brought out *G. M.: Memories of George Moore*. She also planned a book on African ivories, an autobiography, and a study of Spain. This last project ended in disaster when the young Spaniard she had enlisted as collaborator was arrested and it turned out he was a petty criminal. By the time of this setback she herself had been briefly detained by the Spanish police after she had caused a disturbance on a train. Arrested with her assistant, she was released and then expelled.

From now on the story is a terrible one of decline into increasingly erratic behaviour, ill health and delusion. In some ways it bears comparison with the later years of her near contemporaries Jean Rhys and Nina Hamnett, though she lacked Rhys's genius as a writer, and Hamnett's death, dreadful as it was, falls some way short of the awfulness of Cunard's. Back in London in the spring of 1960, she caused havoc among friends and strangers alike, and after being sent to Holloway Prison was certified insane and transferred to

Holloway sanatorium at Virginia Water, where she stayed for three months. Given a clean bill of health in the following November, she was free to leave, and was soon back in France where she and Hugh Ford, an American academic who had hunted her out with the aim of asking her to co-operate on an account of the Hours Press, set to work on the project which would eventually be published in America in 1969 under the title *These Were the Hours*.

But by now her health, physical and mental, had collapsed. Spectrally thin, she spent long periods alone, drinking and smoking too much, her mind at any time liable to give way. Though there was still money had she tried to obtain it, she treated herself as a virtual destitute, flitting between different hotels, all of them ghastly, and the houses of various long-suffering friends. Eventually, exhausted in body and spirit, she was taken to L'Hopital Cochin, where she died on 16 March 1965.

III.

For much of 1943 Nancy Cunard set to work to put together poems that might form a collection of her work to date. Although her major energies as a writer had turned elsewhere after the publication of *Parallax*, she had by no means abandoned poetry. A pamphlet called simply *Poems Two (1925)* had appeared from the Aquila Press in 1930, and her poem 'To Eat Today', dated Barcelona, 13 September 1938, was printed in the New *Statesman* at the beginning of the following month. But there had been no major collection of her work since 1925. Then, in 1943, Edward Thompson, father of Frank and E. P., and known among family and friends as 'old Edward', suggested to her that she might like to consider gathering together the best of her work and publishing it under the imprint of Ernest Benn, for which publishing house he acted as poetry editor. Thompson's radical sympathies were bound to appeal to her. In 1924, which by coincidence was also the year that E. M. Forster published *A Passage to India*, Thompson had brought out his anti-colonial *Atonement: A Play of Modern India in Four Acts*. He also wrote poetry, and although none of it was much good, OUP was to publish his own collection, *100 Poems*, in 1944.

Sadly, 1944 was the year of his death. It meant that the proposal he and Cunard had discussed at length—often by letter—and which had clearly much encouraged her, in the end came to nothing. This was particularly unfortunate, because by the time of his death she had decided on which poems were to be included in the proposed volume, and the sizeable correspondence between them reveals not only how carefully she revised her work but how insistent she was that much of the earlier verse be discarded. While the letters went to and fro, she was typing out poems and assembling them in the order she favoured. After 'old Edward's' death the typescript of the poems, which had passed into his possession, were collected together and kept with the rest of his papers. They are now housed in the Bodleian. That Trent Editions has had access to them is entirely due to the kindness of Dorothy Thompson, to whom we are very grateful.[10]

In preparing this edition I decided against reprinting all of Nancy Cunard's poems. Instead, I have chosen to follow her own wishes and publish the poems she wanted to see preserved. She was not an outstandingly good poet. Edgell Rickword's telling phrase, that poetry was to her an 'uncongenial idiom', gets near to the heart of the matter; she lacked either the ability or, more likely, patience to eradicate those flaws Pound identified in her work. On the other hand, her imagination was undoubtedly stirred into life by political issues on which she hastened to take sides—and the side she took was invariably the just one. This had nothing to do with political correctness. It was born out of a grieved perception that much was rotten in the society of which she was a part, and her own privileged status gave her both an important vantage point to see just how rotten that was and the opportunity to make whatever amends she could. As Henry Crowder in particular came to realise, this occasionally led her to confuse individual with cause. But she was no Mrs Jellyby. Her friends, and there were many, seem to have loved her, and for all her tantrums and imperious moments—she couldn't entirely shrug off the circumstances of her birth and upbringing—she was clearly a most loveable woman. A brave and a good one, too, and one whose generosity of vision and instinct make themselves felt in her poetry as in all else she wrote and did. It is enough.

John Lucas

Notes
1. Anne Chisholm, *Nancy Cunard* (London: Sidgwick and Jackson 1979), pp. 46 and 49.
2. For more on this see my book, *The Radical Twenties: Writing, Politics and Culture* (Nottingham: Five Leaves Publications, 1997, New York, Rutgers University Press, 1999), pp. 137-41.
3. Chisholm, p. 76.
4. Edgell Rickword, *Essays and Opinions 1921-1931* (Cheadle Hulme: Carcanet, 1974), p. 39.
5. Chisholm, pp. 98-99.
6. *T. S. Eliot: The Waste Land: A Facsimile and Transcript*, ed. Valerie Eliot, (London: Faber, 1971), p 27.

7. Peter Ackroyd, *T. S. Eliot* (London: Abacus/Sphere Books, 1985), p 87.
8. Chisholm, p 339.
9. *Authors Take Sides on the Spanish War* was published under the auspices of *Left Review*. For more on this see Andy Croft, *Comrade Heart: A Life of Randall Swingler* (Manchester: Manchester University Press, 2003), pp. 67-69.
10. The letters between Nancy Cunard and Edward Thompson concerning the proposed collection of the poems are, like the typescripts of the poems themselves, housed with the Thompson papers in the Bodleian Library.

Further Reading

Works by Nancy Cunard

Poetry

Outlaws (London: Elkin Matthews and Marrot, 1921)
Sublunary (London: Hodder and Stoughton, 1923)
Parallax (London: Hogarth Press, 1925)
Poems Two (1925) (London: Aquila Press, 1930)
Relève into Maquis (Derby: Grasshopper Press, 1944)
Man=Ship=Tank=Gun=Plane. A Poem (London: np, 1944).

A reprint of *Parallax* (1925) has been produced by Parataxis Editions (Cambridge, 2001).

Poetry by Cunard also appeared in the following collections edited by her, *Henry-Music* (Paris: The Hours Press, 1930) and *Poems for France: Written by British Poets on France since the War* (London: La France Libre, 1944). The latter also appeared in a French translation, *Poèmes à la France* (Paris: Pierre Seghers, 1944).

Other Works

These Were the Hours: Memories of My Hours Press, Reanville and Paris, 1928-1931, ed. with a Forword by Hugh Ford (Carbondale: Southern Illinois University Press, 1969).
G.M.: Memories of George Moore (London: Rupert Hart-Davis, 1956).
Grand Man: Memories of Norman Douglas (London: Secker and Warburg, 1954).
The White Man's Duty: An Analysis of the Colonial Question, with George Padmore (London: W. H. Allen, 1942).
ed. *Authors Take Sides on the Spanish Civil War* (London: Left Review, 1937).
Negro: An Anthology (London: Wishart & Co, 1934).

Black Man and White Ladyship, An Anniversary (London: The Utopia Press, 1931).

A collection of *Cunard's Essays on Race and Empire* has been edited by Maureen Moynagh (Peterborough, Ontario and Orsmkirk, Lancs.: Broadview Press, 2002).

Works about Nancy Cunard

Scant attention has been paid to Cunard's poetry, although the following may be of interest for the additional light they shed on other aspects of Cunard's life and work:

Sheri Benstock, *Women of the Left Bank* (Austin: University of Texas Press, 1986).
Ann Chisholm, *Nancy Cunard* (London: Sidgwick and Jackson, 1979).
Susan Stanford Friedman, 'Nancy Cunard', in *The Gender of Modernism*, ed. Bonnie Kime-Scott (Bloomington: Indiana University Press, 1990), pp. 63-67.
Maureen Moynagh, 'Cunard's Lines: Political Tourism and its Texts', *New Formations* 34 (Summer, 1998), 70-90.

Poems

PRAYER

Oh God, make me incapable of prayer,
Too brave for supplication, too secure
To feel the taunt of danger. Let my heart
Be tightened mightily to withstand pain,
And make me suffer singly, without loss.
Now let me bear alone the ageing world
On firmer shoulders than the giant Atlas.
Make me symbolically iconoclast,
The ideal Antichrist, the Paradox.

(1914)

ADOLESCENCE

I am in years almost the century's child,
At grips with still the same uncertainty
That was attendant to me at the school.
The classics set before us, twenty voices
Took up enunciation, I was dumb—
Then goaded by the teacher's stony finger
Trembling arose to read a meagre essay.
Next History went by, its wars and glories,
And politics that fill young minds with dust
Of Corn-Laws and Reform—severe decades
When England topped the century with Victoria.
But we might never know Queen Catherine
Who ruled imperiously adventurous Russia,
Nor hear the Borgias' crimes, the Papal swindles;
For us no pages on the Medicis,
No panorama of past things in Rome,
But thorny sums, and German verbs rapped out.
For Art we had the photographic torsos
Of Jove and all his Venuses, with words
That lay less easy on the lecturer's tongue:
We never doubted that her themes were Whitman,
Browning and Wordsworth—here we had examples,
Morals and principles.. "Now these two terms
Must be explained to show you've understood."
The winter spent at this came Tennyson.
By half-past twelve all done the rest would go
With confident memories but I forgetful
Scattered the lesson's fragments in the street,
And hated life, with adolescent sense
Of wrong that dallies with tearful introspection.
I knew I could not *learn*, despite the prize
Between my hands the day that I was free.

That summer went in solitude, with thoughts
Humming in concourse as the thronging stars
Appear before the eyes of travellers
Descending to new lands on hurrying feet.
If at some time each man says "World is mine",
Then doubtless rang that clamour in my heart,
And many a fire was lit and worshipped there
Ascetically, with pride, and so with longing.
I held the very world's perplexities,
Throbbing of questions, stirring of heart's blood,
Urging I know not what, till dawn had come.

A year of riot grew, with carnivals,
Music and wine beneath the million lamps
That flanked the thresholds of advancing war.
There were no ruins yet; each hour was gold
That reddened in the fire of its adventure—
Then had I thought of aftermaths and stood
Uncertainly between the opened gates
Scanning the crossroads of a violent world.

                                                    (1915)

ALLEGORY

Hear your three symbols of today:
The lamb, the crow, the eagle live,
The crow would bear the lamb away
Fierce-taloned to a falconry:
Gaunt as the eagle would he strive.

The lamb, the crow, the eagle brood
On temporal sorrows; peregrine
Falls to the snare, and I have seen
Raven lamenting in a wood,
And the lone lamb upon the green.

The lamb, the crow, the eagle die;
The lamb must bleed in merciless hands,
The crow decays on shipwrecked sands,
The eagle exiled from his sky—
So did my only eagle die.

(1922)

MEDITERRANEAN—FROM THE VAR

1

Red earth, pale olive, fragmentary vine
Mellow with sun's decline.
In aftermath of harvest all the days
Are flushed with stillness, lit with almond greys,
And this November afternoon I see
Cypress against the sky so very still.
Upon a narrow strand
Full surges moving to the barren land
Towered with rocks, and on this sudden hill
I pause before the sunset that shall be
In its last hour a psalm
Sped to the journeying heart that seeketh balm.

2

Pale moon, slip of malachite
Above the smoke of the clouds poising
In a green moment that will not last—
And you there, far beyond the furthest roads and sea-paths,
Distiller of the heavens,
One drop of blood in the sky suffusing it:
Sunset, advancing
From this grey weather suddenly.

(1921)

TWO SEQUENCES FROM "PARALLAX"

Dry moss, grey stone, hill ruins, grass in ruins
Without water, and multitudinous
Tintinnabulations in the poplar leaves;
A spendrift dust from desiccated pools,
Spider in draughty husk, snail on the leaf—
Provence, the solstice.
And the days after
By the showman's travelling houses, the land caravels
Under a poplar; the proud grapes and the burst grape-skins.
Arles in the plain, Miramas after sunset-time
In a ring of lights,
And a pale sky with a sickle moon.
Thin winds undress the branch, it is October.
And in Les Baux, an old life slips out, patriarch of eleven
                              inhabitants:
"Fatigué", she said, a terse beldam by the latch,
"Il est fatigué, depuis douze ans toujours dans le même coin."

                In Aix what's remembered of Cézanne?
A house to let (with studio) in a garden.
Meanwhile "help yourself to these ripe figs, *profitez*,
And if it doesn't suit, we, Agence Sextus, will find you
                              another just as good."
The years are sewn together with thread of the same story:
Beauty picked in a field, shaped, recreated,
Sold and despatched to distant municipality—
But in the master's town merely an old waiter, crossly:
"Of course I knew him, he was a dull silent fellow,
Dead now."
And beauty walked alone here,
Unpraised, unhindered,
Defiant, of single mind,
And took no rest, and has no epitaph.

" —- Then I was in a train in pale clear country
By Genoa at night where the old palatial banks
Rise out of vanquished swamps,
Redundant—
And in San Gimignano's towers where Dante once ..
And in the plains with the mountains' veil
Before me and the waterless rivers of stones—
Siena-brown with Christ's head on gold,
Pinturicchio's trees on the hill
In the nostalgic damps, when the maremma's underworld
Creeps through at evening.
Defunct Arezzo, Pisa the forgotten—
And in Florence, Banozzo
With his embroidered princely cavalcades,
And Signorelli, the austere passion.
Look: Christ hangs on a sombre mound, Magdalen dramatic
Proclaims the tortured god. The rest have gone
To a far hill. Very dark it is, soon it will thunder
From that last rim of amaranthine sky.
Life broods at the cross's foot,
Lizard and campion, star-weeds like Parnassus grass,
And plaited strawberry leaves;
The lizard inspects a skull,
You can foretell the worm between the bones.

          (I am alone. Read from this letter
That I have left you and do not intend to return.)

Then I was walking in the mountains,
And drunk in Cortona, furiously,
With the black wine rough and sour from a Tuscan hill,
Drunk and silent between the dwarves and the cripples
And the military in their intricate capes
Signed with the Italian star.
Eleven shuddered in a fly-blown clock—
Oh frustrations, discrepancies,
I had you to myself then ….."
                                        (1923)

SIMULTANEOUS

At one time
The bottle-hyacinths under Orvieto—
At one time
A letter a letter and a letter—
At one time, sleepless,
Through rain the nightingale sang from the river island—
At one time, Montparnasse,
And all night's gloss,
Splendour of shadow on shadow,
With the exact flower
Of the liqueur in its glass.
       Time runs,
            But thought (or what?) comes
Seated between these damaged table-tops,
Sense of what zones, what simultaneous time-sense?

       … Then in Ravenna
The dust is turned to dew
By moonlight, and the exact
Splayed ox-feet sleep that dragged the sugar-beet
To dry maremmas
       Past Sant' Apollinare,
       Fuori Mura.

    In Calais Roads
The foam-quilt sags and swells,
Exact are the land's beacons to the sea—
Twin arms crossed, thrown across sleep and a night-wind.
Time falls from unseen bells
On Calais quays (that were sometimes a heart's keys.)

Red bryony
Steeps in loose night-air, swelling—
October crumples the hedge—
Or the wind's in the ash, opening the seed-pods.
   (The revolution in the weeds—
    Rain somewhere. Rain suggests
   Their dissolution to the seeds.)

   Midnight,
While some protract their trades
Forcing the line—sleep takes them.
But the baker
Cools at the sill, yeast raising auburn flour.

   Midnight
And trains perambulate (*o noctis equi*);
Faust is in hell that would have stopped the horses of night
In their gallops, that would have galloped atop of them,
But was outpaced, overthrown for too exact questioning.

   And in Albi
Les orguilleux sus des roues continuellement
              (hell's fading fresco),
And in Torcello
The mud-fogs now, and on all unknown
Ripe watery wastes
The rich dead silence.

Silence—- or a night-wind on a lawn
Turning the pages one by one of a forgotten book.
                    (1924)

IN PROVINS

So he ran out knocking down the brigadier—
Mince alors: said the officers to each other
In the hotel at the end of the Sunday meal, *fumant la pipe*.

And rain ran in new ditches
Beating on sooty walls where the ramparts are falling
In Provins, ville-haute—with the gale up the winter's watery veins
In clipped crooked fields—wind in the nerves of winter
(The black branches)—in the streets' draughty funnels.

Next morning the lieutenants cantered out in clear sunlight
Past the Jardin Public, a place of shallow waters rising.
What is left of old carvings…seamed fragments in an odour of violets,
And from a café crept the unexplained scent of frezias.
Sun descends on the streams, travelling down the green water.
Against écarlate de Gand and bleu de Nicole they matched their *ners*, noir
                                                                de Provins,
Famous cloth, fast-dyed in the Durteint, hard river-water.
And Abelard
In these level meadows for two years was teaching.
And Thibaut leaned
From the high-town over a murmuring valley,
Thibaut, lord and love-singer who ordered the walls and a monastery.
Word and gesture all one now, dispersed by the unrecording wind,
Other footsteps now, patterning the soundless mould.

Dome on the sunset, blue dome on high hill-distance
Where the ramparts are falling—only a Caesar's tower
Catches the wind still and the rain's minute deteriorations.
The moon collects on puddle-water—
Lilac and prune-flush, suffusions then shadows of nightfall,
Wing-rustle in quickset…and suddenly that hunting-music,
Delaying chords of horns, suspended chords
After silence.

All day I have had memories coming back at me with their gesture of
meetings and partings,
And the sense of some moment in this place that is a memory to be.

By the roadside, what's past…Then the *now* with its hotel bedroom
Where one traveller replaces another—one traveller the abstraction of all—
Time's seasons or shadows put forward, remembered in the wall-paper—
Sad spring still frigid, summer with flies, then the harvests beyond the
octroi,
And the long sheet of winter wrinkled and knotted with branches…

After the soldiers…shuffle and stamp in the clotted sawdust…the
commercial gentry:
'Splendeurs et Misères'? Mais mon vieux, tu n'es pas de ton temps!

Written in Provins,   Published in *Poems Two*
Feb. 1925. France.   Aquila Press, 1930, London.

LOVE'S ALBA AGAINST TIME, TIME'S AGAINST LOVE

Time counts the lovers' strokes,
Each, stringing his knots along endeavour.
Devil—what have I to say to thee?
Wij beminnen elkander…
    we love, love, we love on, in dutch, so.
Who *says* unsays much later;
Who *all* unsays has all said once.
O n c e ? Is that treachery or is it time?

De fil en aiguille, au fil de l'heure…
Filles et fils de l'heure, écoutez:
"Il y eut une fois"…Ay, that's my enemy,
"Once a time", "ago",
And as Aragon has it
"Aima, ai-ma"—
You need no other histories.

So in the blue room
What's mine's yours, ours, in fief holden
For that himself Time is;
So it's not "you and I", it's Time's sport…

Time's foe, my friend,
Gin, the white king—
In his ermines lives possibility,
His card-houses are my Spanish castles
To which the thread of Ariadne is
    What will have been.

Time like a Mexican, a mask on a desert;
The desert full of sacrificial round-stones well-blooded,
Not seen, sensed only, tenants of the long unfinished poem—
Better a stroph or two in honour of the white king:
Oh gin, white king… oh what a lordly lover…
Making much of nothing…wrap oh wrap me into your ermines…..

And here's your shaving-water and your shoe-trees,
Braces and pommatum and your watch and key chains,
Also nine o'clock, sir, all safe sir—
   but not your lover, sir—

                  (1929)

LOVE, DEATH, TIME, WEATHER

so's your Englishman—
O go-for-a-sailor as it's peace-time,
And shatter the context of the blue-red-white.
Say, do they touch at Colon, do they fetch up in the Toulon Darse?
They do, they swing about—and it's up to you.
After so many other afters is there no now?

But I don't think the Poste Restante
Changes our inner geographies nor yet heals hearts,
Much, nor yet do time's heels
Properly leaden heart's spring buds under, nor now nor finally.
Man, your brief uncoiled ache flips back into place like a curl.
  —Three, four… will my love come?
Late late, on morning's wings
A-mourning what's got, not held.
What's held?
That hand on the bed-cover, that's surely a finality,
In visible focus, punkt—
Held, or for later? (such things have been.)

Had I no love I'd a-many,
I'm wrongly angrooved—
Eve and I of myself, how did I come to live in this place,?
Shifting zones of the centre!

(But the north-wings calmy nebulate round the Philippine rice-gods—
This stamp to what collector?)

                                                    (1929)

BETWEEN TIME AND ETC

Living in the past and the future
I see barrages and heart-breakings,
Sameness running by sameness, defied by difference,
Difference overcome, etc.

ETC's large, is omnipresent;
The coming and going of ETC (new god).
What to think—and to whom hand it?
Yet Time is hardly ETC.;
Through with time soon, on with ETC.

We depend on a word
..Dijon..Gueret..for our thought-lines, our Marches and summers.
On "Aima, or how-would-it-have-been granted certain considerations?"
On "I lay in a field and thought to go further",
On "the perfect sonnet",
On "death November 6"—and deaths that are to be.
For before all "a synchroneous comprehension of things" is it not?
One hand on the telephone, one opening, say, a bill,
When the fact of each death first…
No need for pondering what you know and they must guess,
The gaps between, ghost-llines.

All of it so much one thing and another—
So in Venice
That repository of old ships
And the fan-bridge—if you linger by dates.
Everywhere the
Ephemeridae of nights, alone and not alone.

Beginning with Dowson, then "in Timon's rage",
Having it out with love and time…
Are we the real?
Started out of utmost improbability,
Putting it mainly between asterisks, falling into metres,
In a time of waiting (dost ever know any other time?)
I knew the apparent sweet and sharp of the lives of others,
Such obstinate credos as wave on wave,
The never samely repeated BLANK of each spring—

O landscape of the green field, gin bottle and intention,
Next year's hot foot with his "As you were!"

(1929)

TELL IT, GLEN

They lie, all those who say "The world is beautiful
Because it holds all things and time runs still
Over the crowns and corpses, both are one to him,
Sorrow and joy are one, for no man has his will."

They lie, such times they say "We cannot bring
Disharmonies to concord, wars must be
Part of our progress, growth, machinery,
Strengthening our manhood, as one lops a tree."

They lie, who say "Look for it to the sky,
Your happiness, life is a swathe of pain."
They fail, who fashion then an ivory tower
With pride of despair or shuttering-in of brain.

Hast ever seen one climb an ivory tower
That has to work at filling every hour
With speed-up goods? And in the hours between
Shuffles his thoughts with heavy footsteps where
The sudden earth's a soft or sullen green
By pathways to the pits, where that first flower,
When flowers come, seems half a bitterness,
Almost an idler's jibe—For who can use
Such as a joy who must be counting: shoes,
Miles, wages, dole, cuts, lay-off, mother's face:
"Go back tomorrow, son"—and at that place
Pass this untroubled bud of liberty...
Did 'God' make man? Woman and man made me;
'God' must have made the flowers, for they are free;
Not I.

A living poet tells of one long dead,
A footloose singer came on spring's first flower,
So blue it brought him tears for her who'd lain
Her body by another's in that year,
That once was his, no longer now—He said
Merely: "It was so blue, it was herself again."

We do not weep for love: we call for life,
— Let love come if it will—for meat and bread,
Man's due and common rights; yes, and time to be
Aware of being alive before we're dead.

Down in those mines under the sea itself.
Do you know what we look like, people, at twenty-three,
Some of us? Hollow-faced, ashen, sombre and scarred,
Lop-sided, shuffling, tooth-rotted—people, that's me.

Glen is my name, Northumberland—out of work.
I did the Hunger March in thirty-four.
Now sit and think: no job. The dole drips pence.
Do I conclude: "Life's this" or "Is there more?"

(1934)

AND ALSO FAUSTUS

Faust longed for a new world
And got it—
Ran through the transmogrifications of the pure intellect, its philosophies
and appetites,
And came to the end of it.
Come death, take me—quoth. Or was it the mercenary old deil's contract
that called "time"?
Whichever, it's a despair-story.

What do you think, would Faustus have gotten it clear *now*?
Hitler would have destroyed him 'with honours':
"Powerful man that…Make it a resounding example…"
He couldn't have enregimented Doctor Faustus.

What do you think, would the Doctor have come down into the street,
As we say in France,
Preluded with laughter the vacillations of the bewildered intellectuals
(As no doubt he does now)
And set them his teasers?

Yet the Doctor could be claimed as the highest of the honourable ivory
towers,
Gone in the head with too much study in the chase of the absolute…
(Claim him, thus will you never hold him.)

I think the Doctor would have come down into the street
In his black velvets with a touch of red at the throat
And fallen in step somewhere between the old seared comrades and the
young.

You wouldn't have heard him sing but it's he would have swung the singing,
You mightn't have seen him, that ageless and timeless, but very much *there*,
The kind that deflects a bullet-on-the-way from its mark.
They can't kill *him* anyway, and what he means…..

How often History is a cruel march; how easily a desert becomes a
cataclysm—
How often this year I think: Les morts et Faust avec nous.

(To Tristan Tzara, after his great speech on "The Meaning of the Poem in
Life", at the 1st Writers' Congress in Defence of Culture, June 24, 1935, in
Paris.)

(1935)

YES, IT IS SPAIN

What is a bomb?
Something I can't yet believe.
What is a tomb?
Something I can't yet see.
And what is a wound in its wounding,
And the shot cutting a vein and the blood coming
Out of an eye, say, stabbed—are these things too for me?

Bitter, how bitter, do you remember in a certain by-now long ago,
Anger boiling through in tears on the foul London midnight stain.
18, 18, 18—if a man, yes, I'd have been shifted over into it then,
Into the great-to-do, the last one, the Grande Guerre,

With some cross-eyed crossroad finger pointing at me
"On!" on to some bottomless pit for the long waiting and wondering:
"Can you tell me *what it's about?*" till the hour's coming
With its "Ready for death?" "Hell no—ready for nothing"… that's me.

You, man, mumbling that misplaced, ridiculous "a spot of bother",
O brother contemporary, and some of you the salt of the earth—
What else could you do but go? We shall not forget you,
(And that's fact, humanly not officially said),
Nor forgive the present Flanders-Poppy flaunting ahead towards the next
one,
By La-Der-des-Ders into La Prochaine. I have not forgot my dead.

You think this is something new? No; this too becomes Spain,
All of it, all of it's Spain, with the dial set at Revenge—
No past pageantry of wan mothers and lovers weeping,
Ruined, undone for ever, that Spain cannot avenge.

I'm of a mood tonight, boy, marked DO NOT TOUCH,
Though somebody, say, like Villon, may have the best of it,
Long dead and safe from the shells and cries and wounds,
And the scythes of war mowing ground for our latter-day tombs.

I'm of a mood with Bosch and Zola and Villon,
Who brooked no nonsense, who wrote and painted and said
Their NO against foolery, NO against lying, their NO to
The proud-fleshed fakir, their NO to the living-dead,

The popes and imposters, the critics pragmatic, the pomps—to
Prick irony into function by use of the heart and the fact—
Into the washtub with History, for the better showing of it;
Then, now, à la mode du temps—that the artist becomes the act.

Blake too—you'll do well to remember that naked man's announcement:
"It is impossible, yes, for truth to be told *so's understood*
And not be believed". Great Blake is the Day of Judgement,
Vengeful, oppressive, peculiar—Blake's all to the good.

Daddy Hogarth, and Faust, Shakespeare, Chaucer and Marlowe,
Goya, Heine and Daumier, and the long-exiled giant, Hugo,
Dante—what do you think they'd say to you, artist in hesitations?
Shall I call on these our dead for their answer? "Go,

Learn from the day's ruins and tombs" they say, "our trust's in the people
Who fought against iron, Church and Bank, with naked fist, fight not in
vain—
Every man to his battle, child; this is yours, understand it,
In that desert where blood replaces water—Yes, it is Spain."

(1937)

TO EAT TODAY

In Barcelona today's
air-raid came as we were
sitting down to lunch after
reading Hitler's speech
in Nüremberg. *The Press.*

They come without siren-song or any ushering
Over the usual street of man's middle day;
Come unbelievably, abstract, beyond human vision,
Codicils, dashes along the great maniac speech—
"Helmeted Nüremberg nothing", said the people of Barcelona,
The people of Spain—"*ya sabemos*, we have suffered all."

You heroes of Nazi stamp, you sirs in the ether,
Sons of Romulus, Wotan—is the mark worth the bomb?
What was in it? salt, and a half-pint of olive,
Nothing else but the woman, she treasured it terribly,
Oil for the day folks would come, refugees from Levante,
Maybe with greens…one round meal…but you killed her,
Killed four children outside, with the house, and the pregnant cat.
Hail, hand of Rome, you passed—and that is all.

I wonder—do you eat before you do these things,
Is it a cocktail or is it a pousse-café?
Are you sitting at mess now saying "Visibility, medium.
We got the port or near it with half a dozen", I wonder—
Or highing it yet on the home-run to Mallorca,
Cold at 10,000 up, cursing a jammed release…
"Give it 'em, *puta Madonna*, here, over Arenys—
Per Bacco, it's nearly two—bloody sandwich it's made down there—
Aren't we going to eat today, *teniente*? Te-niente?"
Driver in the clouds fuming, fumbler unstrapping death.
You passed; hate traffics on; then the shadows fall.

On the simple earth
Five mouths less to feed tonight in Barcelona.
On the simple earth
Men trampling and raving on an edge of fear.
Another country arming, another and another behind it—
Europe's nerve strung like catapult, the cataclysm roaring and swelling…..
But in Spain no. Perhaps and Tomorrow—in Spain it is HERE.

(Written during the air-raid of Sept 13, 1938, in the Hotel Majestic,
Barcelona.)

PAMIATNIK—MEMORIAL OF BITTERSWEET

This is the place
Of indescribable expression, like the look on the face of a certain morning.
This is the house
Where so much of much, so much of nothing happens.
This is the day
And the night
And the dawn
And the tear
Coming out of the wine or the heart temporarily sterile.
This is the place of near-despair, the crucible of world-sorrows.
This is the place
Of the news-letter bleeding out a lynching;
Cell of ferocity, seam of defeat, zone of continuation.
This is the place of Spain-my-Spain—
These agonies, laced with individual sorrows.

This is the house of time withering away,
And time running, and time at a loss,
Like a foot forever on the stair, and the return of dying called winter.
It is no place of linked easy lovers;
Its temper is bitter-sweet, its pulse is called poetry,
Its heart is a roaring red, its conscience intransigent.
(O it can be soft and sweet too—how long how long, my darling?)
Here often sits December, with the wan drip of the month
Giving the black-out, when the peasants play at Brueghel on the roads.
It can hate and love and scorn in one, it is cruel;
It is a roaring red, I said, under its proud-necked sufficiency.
It sits in judgement on the creeping and racing of the century
Under the warring flags of victories and assassinations
And the waves rising and rising
Of the wrath of outraged humanity—
Judges, and fiercely finds wanting.

There is nothing we can do for it, nothing, oh nothing;
It hates us, it hates us, it hates us—
It is like me,
It is like life.   (1937)

EOS

Come spring there might be armistice
Between half-loving warring two—
Can truth evolve from travesty?
I think our first's our last solstice.

He will he will not, both—which most?
All-inconsistent, true to plan;
Take it or leave it while you may—
This is a three-in-the-morning man.

Between the book and bottle move,
The poltergeist is at the bar;
A "portrait of the man I love"?
Oh hound that bays an icy star.

Aurora boreal was our sign,
The red in the night explaining fear,
The drunken burn, the knife in the air,
The pashing mire and January wine.

Lie in this bed while yet you may,
Get you your most and I will mine;
To kill and to remake each day,
Such was part-lesson of the vine.

Kiss that holds not how should a tear?
Without the wave there is no strand.
What be these siltings in your earth,
This foreign body in my land...

What price the candle, what, the prize?
Act 1—and last. The month has gone
Wasting fine substance every day;
We talk, we doubt; the hackles rise.

Meanwhile all fate climbs to the roof
Watching the iron cars grind on
And echoes: Heil. The Vienna strings
Are snapped, the iron chord bears down.

So died one land, while private spate
Of scorn and sweet ran hot and chill,
The spring of 1938
Marched, and the omens boded ill.

Sophisticate or simple man,
All's one; fate nears with drilling feet—
Oh shambles shambles of the heart,
"How fares in there? The world's in it".

The world, cross-currented, a-glow,
Identified that while with you ...
We ate our lotus there a month—
"No other taste shall change this..." *No?*

No other taste? Deliverer time
Writhes in the bud and waits the spring.
But lovers' bird a phoenix is,
Half-crazed with hope; on dazzling wing

It rides the flurry of the Horn—
Think you we'll round those furious tides?
The look-out man still calls: She rides!
Hush on his daring until port.

When's that, and where—Volubilis?
How comes to me a name like this,
Lure with same nothing at the end,
Stage on the road I-hit-I-miss?

∧   ∧   ∧

Volubilis stands yet on sand
In Africa with its Roman twist
That time wrecked too, that death has kissed—

Ay, that's the lotus never-land.

(1938-1943)

SEQUENCES FROM A LONG EPIC ON S P A I N

1

It begins in Morocco, under the long-depressed Crescent,
With a voice in the night: "Turn out! Manoeuvres!"
And the Moors took
The usual dawn-roads and then—it all got different.
"Had we but known . . for there are paths between the Moroccos;
We could have fled, but we did not know."
Ordered into planes, this, German, that, Italian,
Moors into Spain marched, gun at rib, wondering;
And came
"Into lands of Spain, si señor, us, *Regulares*.
They told us then: 'Fair in Seville; you, Guard of Honour'.
The devil a fair! But threats, blows and secrecy incomprehensible;
A train, a train, *and* a train, and no place with a name, for us.
Then in two weeks
Crashed doubt into truth: WAR. But *whose* war? Now we know.
We are not prisoners. We are deserters to the Republic;
Walked from that place of many arches (Segovia), a woman showed us the way."
Oh Moors of earnest word—you five I saw later in Madrid.

2

It begins, for me, in a Montmartre street with a crazy footstep
Racing, pleading, at midnight: "I *must* talk to someone, you...
Listen, woman: if you knew how close it is,
The horror... Can you stop it? I am an airman; I fell.
It is not that. They'll use me tomorrow again,
And I'll go wherever it be; I'm a commercial flier.
That is not it.
I saw my brother burn in the sky; I was a child,
Near Verdun, near Verdun—1918.
Planes fall, burning. I know hell. Do you know hell?
And now it's coming again...
If you knew, if you knew—so soon—or do you know?

> Gone with the wind of Ethiopia-laden July,
> A scar of a man. What was it, foreknowledge, coincidence?
> And then, in four days, in a roar of flames it began.

19 —— Barcelona —— 19, immortal July.

M a d r i d 1936

I cannot see the landscape for the tears,
But winter has come with snow in the new craters there.
They have died and died in Madrid, perhaps mainly the children;
Look at their pictures, peoples, observe the virtuosity
Of death, the pock-signer, the master in fanciful sameness—
Behold this singular leprosy,
This hither-and-yon of destruction that needs no one *wound*;
The childrens' mouths are open in death,
Is it suspense? No, a finality.
What is the answer to come?
PEOPLES, WHAT IS YOUR ANSWER?

It is winter in the round still parks,
Snow and misery are the temporary new crutches of death—
Only, over the snow fly the words of all Europe now…
Words from the Pacific Americas, words of Antillean temper,
Coming together, comrades—words from Finland to Abyssinia;
The scale fills in, the octave is complete.
They are all here
For Paco, with Paco the espadrilled, once the hod-carrier,
                              now Spain's Red Army man.
Words of men, deeds of men—men here and coming,
Grain cast out of the great seed-bag of man's heart,
Ready seed sown, fallen, moving, risen and proven.
This is the International, Paco—this too is a finality.

December 1936, M a d r i d

By the Manzanares,
And the Parque del Oeste and the Casa del Campo,
By the Puerta de Hierro and the Hill of the Partridges,
University City…Casa de las Flores…Quixote and Pancha in the snow,
(Their statue a front now)…Carabanchél…
By the shards of the southern wasteland,…Arguélles,.Vallécas,
Líria's Palace in rivers of flame…
By the Puente de los Franceses, by the Southern Station,
Cuatro Caminos, Tetuán (the air bursting with death)…
By Úsera, Araváca, Garabítas,
By Las Véntas, Monclóa, Lavapiés,

B a t t l e.

If the poets be not dead—but what matter if the poets be dead—
Nothing matters but Madrid in its winter of death and dying—
Yet the poets were not dead; they came, anguished, wondering, and erect
Men of Madrid and women, and children on road and street
Taught what a clenched fist means when what is in it is truth.

December 1 9 3 7,

They did not pass—through Toledo Gate where only the sunset passes,
(I have seen I have seen)
With the final *Bmmmmm-p* of hand grenades, beholding the smoky battle.
"Not for us, those", said the sentry there. "Now tell us of Major Attlee
Who came here a week ago. Is he true? If so, what will he do for us?"

          … And the smoky battle,
Smudged, an uncertain fresco; how far—a mile? Less than two,
Under Madrid in the snow and gold of December.
Florída, Gran Vía, Telefónica,
Street of Shells, pride of edifices;
Noon a-freeze, then the windy blackout, the deserted midnight,
The moon in a hollow tooth—such, once, were houses—

(Oh heart like a scarlet opal, who shall tell you as befits you?
Men and statues have fallen, a year has passed—but *they* did not pass.)

The Exodus from Catalonia—Republican Spain
walks into France—Jan-Feb 1 9 3 9

For these
France was a virgin field, a page open, ready
To write G r a t i t u d e on, a field for the ploughing-under of pain,
A piece of calm after agony; they came as a gift here;
And so the flocks came, besides the gold and the cars and the chariots
                                                    defeated in hell—
But mostly came the hearts of men.

What was this frontier, tell me?
A pass for flocks,
A transient mile between those final rocks,
A strangulation with a shining end,
Hell's funnel—
      So they saw it, waiting 10,000 deep each day to climb their gehenna.
Somewhere, sometime, between bristled sabres and stamping platoons,
Peace! After the chesty sergeants and General Staff's barking orders across
                                                    their way,
Rest!
      And the Sister Republic answered:
          "*We hate you*".

If these frontier things must be, they thought, next hours must bring
That change when man becomes man again with his lamb at his side,
On the green of earth resting, under an almost Spanish sun.
Climbing gehenna they thought:
Aren't we *seres humanos*—beings, human?
But the frontier—what is a frontier?
"Give us arms to fight or let us in" said the old man trudging down back
                                        to Spain,

Telling me: "Back to Junquera! Turned back!!
What means a 'frontier'? This! Now we search the ground
For any piece of food that might have dropped when we passed before—
Back to Junquera for 'permits'—to enter what? France!
That is what this frontier means: *a line at the end of starvation*,
30 and more months of death, treacheries..all that has been..
72 am I. I was mayor of my place
In Asturias, and many a foul deed have I known,
But this, such as this, never! It is inconceivable.
All night we stood on that line, the 'frontier', in the roar of rain;
I saw a woman give birth on the road, an old man die,
— Something like 3,000 of us there—people fainting, gangrene growing
                                        in wounds…
And now they turn us back. We are looking for food at our feet.
Have you seen anything one could eat? What should we do—ay,
                                    what shall we do?"

I have seen I have seen
All this poor woof and weave, this drapery of exodus
Rotted with rain in one night here, transposed into compost,
A fit bed for the conqueror—along with one pale dead ass,
Les quatre fers en l'air, death's humble and monstrous belly;
Seen many a foul deed done, heard the hearts of men break,
Seen the blood of Spain's truth run dark—but no waste scrap of food.

"It is not right, compañero—they are mad in France, compañero,
Because it's coming to them the same tide;
We should have fought it till victory, we by their side—
But now, back to Junquera, with no crumb of food…"

Is there pardon for France and Franco in this in a mile of centuries?
The triumph of hell nears completion. A whole people has walked away.

(1938-39)

THE LANDS THAT WERE TODAY

(To Kay Boyle)

Ah listen, mark—the Devil's sick again.
It is night; it is Radio; it is the Danzig brew;
Noise of rushing rabble, shingle by arrogant sea,
Hush, hush, the demagogue's rampant.

How interesting, hideous but interesting, the noise of it all,
The key-drop, the holy tear in the voice between hiccups to Mars,
The down-slide, the mad uprush.. "Humanität".. the orchestration.
It's lasted.. "Begeisterung am Menschen".. already one hour—

Here in Normandy
The stooks are set, the men gone in their millions to the East.

"Sie wissen hier genau"—oh voice of Devil-never-Fausted-with-doubt—
We do, *genau* we do—the land that was Heine and Goethe.
Do not cutt off the man's voice, pray, with your sticks to the fire,
Plague on your cooking-clatter; *listen*: a dictator bursts.

I am thinking: "After the countries, he killed himself; yes, he could try that,
But that is not enough; nothing can be enough."

… The land that was…Today "finalism" without meaning.

On the wings of wine I am thinking, thinking, thinking,
Past-present-future, of something that will not go into words.
Tears have told it, tears buried with blood in revenge pendent in Italy,
Something…how does it go … something like a quotation:
"How long, how long,
Dictator's stamping-ground the people's breast?"

What do we know of war? We know there is some kind of war,
Cynical, covert, cold, censored, a wraith-war, leashed holocausts,
There in men's East—but here, later, with lilacs, acacias,
Plaited round batteries, snapped—bleeding spring over corpses,

over one I knew?
My village, my lovely land, my bit of eternal France…..

Listen, tune in again, for the set is ending:
"Three years, says Britain. I, Hitler, answer, seven!
Siegheil!" (Oh their raucous hall and their gruff teutonic band)
And that is that,

and …

And then the Gallic cock lifted his spur
And the old lion woke out of his cynic rheums
And shook his claws, brushed fur and came alive again.
And all the tense driven pageantry of Empire got under way,
And we are forty now that knew the day
They killed Edward, Patrick, Ramond, Ivo, and my lover
In such fields' corners that are less England ever than is a stoop of mull

by September stove—
Ay, it begins again, but it is different, for there are wars, and more, between;
And I have seen, I have seen,
Lived part of one, and shall again, I know;
And been
Where truth haunts rock and stone immortally round a people strong

in the thigh;
I have seen them fight, and the fear of their truth used as order that

they should die.

And now, dead men of England, lend me your ears
By the autumn stove, and from your timeless close,
Your chartless regions and unknowable spheres,
Communicate, pass by, or whisper what no man knows:
Is Humanity inching along? Is it 'Now", is it "Not in our time"?
We are at one on it all—we are at one I suppose…

(Sept. 1939)

JOURNEY TO THE NEW WORLD

You, *mijito*, my son, my lover, my son,
You are free now, *free*…you that went to kill bulls in Avila
And found the priests with their guns there, the black snake with its head
up.
You are free—free to grieve still, but free to *live* again too.
We have left Europe, changed the North Star for the Southern Cross.
Look! Here it all begins. It begins at Mendoza,
After the weary wonder of the Pampas in the Argentine's dustrobe—
We drank beer without cease crossing them, thought of nothing as far
                                        as that's possible…
Look! Here it begins. We are in it. It has begun.

What does it mean, this note scribbled in the crazy car
Curvetting through a grey dawn, these words: "The two passes—Exodus?"
I remember—the Pass of death, the Pyrenean; the Pass to life, the Andes;
The Andes, the Andes, the Andes—that is a name for life.
And then:
"Desprecio a la palabra en Europa, a la possia, a la verdad".
You are eloquent my notes of that morning, you say further
(Of the sea-journey and arrival) "It begins and it ends in colours,
Colour of sea in a hostile land, the white on the gray."
Seven days anchored, waiting the convoy in the mouth of the Gironde,
Frozen, benighted, spectral, raging, inarticulate—
Two hours at noon—for a painter, the white on the gray;
But for a poet, these: crispation, paralysis.
Ay, the end of France was the itch and the histoires de géndarmes,
A meet end, with its passes and permits, to a life there of twenty years.
Start of the passage to the New World, the note says:
"Exit, suspended in pallor, pastels, Impressionists."
We had Life-Belt and Life-Boat drill one day, the crew with gas-masks,
A paternal captain and 172 scared Portuguese emigrants;
We had Lisbon at coaling-time, the black devils enacting hell
With their spades and buckets, and the roar of the coal down the shute;
Cents a day for this, 20. We had Casablanca, Dakar,
Arab misery, giant Senegal, with Goree, past womb of pain;
Here the slaves came in their coffles, from here was "the Middle Passage"—
Today the old fort, the Slave-House, at last it is empty.

Dakar, foul with colonial purport, resplendent with Negro strength.
Days and more days—then the Equator,
A lake of milk and mirages and birds that were flying fish.
We had Rio—oh New World, you first at Rio..
Went ashore in a blast of Carnival, devoured you, adored you;
And Santos—oh harbours and tropics in a beauty that never ends.
And in Montevideo, friends, and the colours of Spain-my-Spain;
Another colour: waters of the Rio Plata before Buenos Aires;
It is the opal again, but a tawny and turbid opal, not that of Madrid.

The car—it is in the Andes now, and the note staggers:
"It ends with this, the Grand Approach,
It ends in Chile, with freedom.
Look! Here is the miracle,
And light on the miracle;
The light, you can almost touch it.
A cactus grows in the snow here, when it is the time of snows.
Look! These are cactii in the deep of the bend..
Look! Here are horses and no man near them,
For the horses here, they are wild, they are wild, they are free.
And then the great line of the summits, look, at the top of a curve,
Older than all the gods of earth, surging up at one go,
One higher than all the rest—all saying 'Eternity'.
Can we leave our pain at the foot here, of the eternal snows
Where the highest says 'Behold me: I am Aconcagua'?"

How many miles have we come? Here are no miles, only time,
Only continuance and colour mating with colour.
And then a note says:
"Glück in a field composed, sometimes,
In a green field, on his piano, with golden wine
And bird-song and wind over flowers, and made such rhymes
And waves of sound all hearers wept with ecstasy…"
Why do I think of Glück here—it is because of that, the ecstasy.
The Andes are singing to me; they are sound made visible, there are words
even in a message,
They pull me, they hold me, they say: "Stay, you are part of us".

And where are we now? In Uspalláta, the sole man-made in all of this,
A tawny road reeling, an inn with waters and the *sauce llorón.*
It is almost noon, and the car bounds on again—
And then and then, tell me my note, what did you say?
"I have *seen* noon here, noon burst open in all its colours,
Colour, eternal as stone by the Tomb of the Inca -
The colours change every few miles...
There is water here too, the Rio Mendoza."
There is water...Here raged the waters of avalanche, the *aluvión.*
Destruction monumental on a scale with the Andes,
A few years back. And the driver said: "Here too
Passed the armies of Liberation, General San Martin, and the emancipation
                                        of the two countries
From the tyrant Spain."
And my last note says:
"What is this frontier, tell me?
The Pass to Eternity—"

The journey is near its end—height carved out in rock, ridge upon ridge,
A little train in a world of stone, descent into a green world, trees, maize
                                        and water;
You are in Chile, *mijito,* you have reached the Promised Land—
All life is a long or a little train,
And weary the heart, the foot-loose heart, the Spanish heart
In its cell, beating and waiting, beating and waiting.
Take freedom today oh heart—for as to me
These things I saw them through a veil of pain...

Of pain, of pain—Ah how it comes
Repeating with a pulse of drums,
And seldom does their rhythm still—
Drums for the knife that's mate to love;
Love is my fate, love is my ill,
My inmost meaning, utmost loss,
My spring, my lock and key, my wild
Ninth wave that rages round your stone—
These things are nothing to you, child,
Maker of pain, undone by pain,
Or are they?
And must the tide and temper of it surge ever so?
Torero, what is your answer?
Or will these eternities we cross give me one?
This is what happens at the meeting of two elements—
There is pain and ferocity, and a measure of love.

What have the drums to do here in Eternity?
Intrusion of Europe's heart-ache, pain has come with us
And travels this road too in his swathe of grief,
And faces Aconcagua.....

    Thus we entered the land of the Condor.

                        (Spring 1940)

CHILE

In January 1939 a cataclysmic earthquake wrecked the town of Chillán, eight hours to the south of Santiago. When I was there a year and a half later, people still stood (in the rain) thinking: "how to rebuild?" Nothing can be more tragic than these ruins. Nothing? That very week the Germans were surging over France, laying new ruins on a gigantic scale. Of these things one would talk with the people of Chillán, and with the warm-hearted *rotos* of Chile. The *roto* is the name given to the poor man of Chile, the descendant of the Indians and the Conquistadores; literally "the broken one". The poet is Arturo Gardoqui, one of Chile's most lyrical poets. I have seen the ruins of the house in which he was buried alive, seen them with him. But soon we were forgetting all this for the anguish of France; it was in June, 1940.

> Innumerable Pompeis of the world,
> This is your limbo, past and yet to be—
> Between these wraths and rains and bumping sea
> Man's hates and furies thrive—with courtesy
> Out of forgotten Spain. But what is furled
> Here in the rock is rock's, not for you, man.
> Was it worth while, Conquistador? Chillán
> Answers: Behold. The latent vagary
> Of quakes commands—come flood, come June—at call,
> Omnipotent, and triumps the *roto*'s will
> In drunken heart's ease..Ah this Chilian still,
> This vat of drink to the lees…Then in it all
> One poet issuing from that January tomb,
> Experience gotten there for future's bomb.

(June 6, 1940.   Concón, Pacific. Chile.)

AMARANTH OF SUNSET

Done, undone, not done, and done too well—
Oh Chile of my despair, oh orb of thieves,
Oh whirlpool madness—oh you curious hell
Of love and hate, you cradle of all that grieves.
All Shakespeare vested in one small drunk man,
All of the poets in this love of mine,
All of the sorrows on that raft of wine;
Was this the man for me, the final man,
Who knows? Gone—to the amaranthyn last
Shaft as he watched it muttering "Never more…"
I see my poet walking by the shore
Of time alone as I, locked in our past,
Snarling, quiescent. And then up speaks the wine:
"You to your life, *mijito*; I, to mine."

(1940)

(*Mijito*: my very dear, a Chillenism)

AT DAWN

No! I will sit and let the iambics play,
And I will wring the sonnet's neck and say
"Hell and eternity have met today
Here—and I, I defy them—come what may,
A stranger in your land, not more, at bay."
And who has ears may listen if so he list,
Nothing will gain, oh nothing; ("amethyst
That keepeth away the fumes of wine", they say).
I will not talk or answer. All of my sphere
Lingers or centres on love that's gone, or here,
How can I tell, here in this transient room?
All is a lie, up to the uttermost tomb.
Nor would I know if all is done and lost—
Dawn is for ice, not for computing cost.

(1940)

PSALM FOR TRINIDAD

I am Trinidad—Columbus discovered me,
Land of the Carib then, land of palm-trees, humming-birds,
I am Africa, India now; gone are slaves and indentured labour,
The sons of these am I, the wage-serfs, under a still-Victorian Union Jack.

    (*Oh de sun de sun ha laash me; it 96 in de shade.*)

I am Oil and the reek and muck of it, the wage lost in the strike,
The worker's rotten barrack, the crusted, festering yard
Where life's not life but simply a six-score hard
Under a tin roof, five or six to a room; life is a sentence here.
80 cents, 60 cents, 50 or 35's my daily pay..
Slums of Empire—have you seen me, Lloyd George, to be calling me that?

    (*What to do wid dis sun? When it not sun in come rain.*)

I am Butler, Uriah Tubal Buzz Butler of the Oilfields,
A brown Negro man who wanted to make it a better life,
Started organising, spoke out, was jailed for it—with the Governor saying:
                                                he is right,
And the Oil Co.s working the police, and the Governor sent away.

    (*Oh Gawd, oh Gawd, what he do, Butler? Butler must come again.*)

I am the cane-brake, the largest sugar-factory in the Empire,
Thin silent folk of India in those fields, dividends, engineers,
Bullock-carts, piety—brown hands splitting the golden cocoa-pods,
African faces in green depths, silent too, wondering "how long dis way?"

    (*40 cents, 20 cents—depend if I man or woman—it so, my day.*)

I am Government House on its official lawn
Facing the Savannah—mine is no easy dawn.
I am Censorship suppressing, controlling, because here there is always fear...
I am the white creole, the planter, paramount among the snobs,
I say it's a happy island, my summum bonum is the cocktail hour.
I am the Police Force and helmeted Colonialism rampant and dominant.

(*Here it get thirty days me for pick one fruit by roadside.*)

I am Calypso, brown bards of the people improvising irony in song;
I am the multitude, the articulate, keen
Brown face and black and gold; the courteous Chinese
Trading in the towns, Indians passing mute almost ghostly;
I am the young hotheads, the cackle of old dark laughter, the ripe
vernacular on the roads..

(*What about after de war, man you think it come the Democracy?*)

I am Duprés, O'Connor, Gomes, Percival and Payne,
I am "The People", the battling mayor of Port of Spain,
I am Kay and "New Dawn", you can read the truth of me in this;
I am Gittens and Comma, brains that hold the import and savour of me.

(*Now dese our friends for true, in deir writings, deir oratory.*)

I am Rienzi, walking between diplomacies,
Politics, politics—the burden sits heavy on me.
I am the poet Cruickshank, my Wordsworthian line
Sweeps oer the world and sculpts it, and I have done my time
In Colour's gusty battles. I am the anonymous force
Of human will, of hope for juster days soon.

(*After de war, man, like for England for Trinity.*)

I am the Iron Music, the fork on the bottle with the spoon,
The drum out of Africa, the tambu-bambu, the collective Carnival;
Always always a note of sadness under the singing,
Always a wistfulness, an uncertainty, a back-bringing…

    (*Dis Carnival here, it our onliest own time in de year.*)

I am this voice in the night—(heard heard in the street):
"Dey call it New Year's Eve—Man, what new year is dis for we?
Workin' man can't eat, can't sleep, can't live properly;
Dis place it have nothin'; dis night it nothin' new for you or me.."

    (*New Year, Old Year, all de same for such as we.*)

    Trinidad, effervescent———
                 look at me, look at me, look at me here.
                        (1941)

"HOW LONG?" IS NOT "FOR EVER"

Come look at us, islands that the Carib tide
Bathes with eternal swell; us, cocoa, palms,
Sugar and pitch and rum and oil—and psalms
Learned under slavery, pulsing yet inside
Men's toilsome breast and woman's. Come eventide
Their angelus outdoes the facts of day;
My dears, you are too good—"please-God"—you pray
For that which is *your due*, and facts outride
All God-ward hopes. Yet "God is our onliest friend"
You say to me. I know this too shall end
When the world's comrades muster to your side;
The planet's workers and the poet's pen,
Take them for allies—Truth is a rising tide—
My Africans, an answer comes to "W h e n ?"

(1941)

LESS THAN THE SLAVE

She stood breast-high..yes, that is it, breast-high,
Faith with a cutlass armed in the still wood,
Amid the alien…yes, transplanted; stood
Saying "If God spare life this ends, and I
Need work no more for twenty cents a day!"
Lily! You knot from Africa! You thing
Less than the slave of old—fill baskets, bring
Cocoa and coffee; pick those beans; *they'll* weigh.
So—you are worth two dimes, and men worth four
In those Antillian glades. Black, ragged, bowed
With agues, tired, illiterate—see their crowd
Dancing the cocoa on the drying-floor,
Democracies? Not here! IS as HAS BEEN—
Rulers, behold the sweet in your machine.

(1941)

In answer to Trinidad's poet who asks me

"....What was it moved you to enlist
In our sad cause your all of heart and soul?"

TO ALFRED CRUICKSHANK

My friend, ship rocks, and seas come great and small
Over the gunwale, but the captain reads
On, despite this. On land the teeming seeds
Breed without fear, and after the gusty fall
Of rain comes ready are they, present, erect,
Grown. Do you sense the symbol in it all?
The man outlives the storm, the tribunal
Of nature judges, tempering the elect.
Our lives are wars—You ask: "Why love the slave,
The 'noble savage' in the planter's grave,
And us, descendants in a hostile clime?"
Call of the conscious sphere, I, nature and man,
Answer you: "Brother, instinct, knowledge…and then
Maybe I was an African one time."

(1941)

14 JUILLET 1941

In the trough of the wave, in the pit, the very nadir
Of all—what's in your sack, Time, for the likes of we :
Fortitude, perseverance, defeats, suspense most horrible, then more
                                                    endurance?
Best that we cannot tell—or would I rather see

The heart of the blackness bared, the ultimate, present whole
At its closest, the total corruption in the skull?
More and more communal is man's grief—yet each tragedy is solitary—
Europe, you sea of pain—how long is this tide at its full?

La Habana, July 14, 1941   Not published

FRANCE

Some truths flame, incandesce—others like the blue
Deep of the timeless fiord, or fires seen through husk of ice,
Wait. Truth is hate. This is France. No other necessity's
Afoot in the corn, in the coal-mine, erect on the castle at Saverne
In the full of the banished tricolor, the one put back there.

France is married to grief, bears grief's brood, is grief's cold widow;
The name of her peace is Death. This, after the breaking of the pulses,
The heart staggered, the brain convulsed, the nerve paralysed.
Somewhere in it all remained the empty zero hour—
Hate enters the zero hour; good. This womb shall bear life again.
Who is hate? She has made him her only lover,
Single in purpose as a magic; as luminous, as multiple as star dust.

Hate like a little familiar animal has the freedom of the house,
The freedom of road and city. There is hate in a sou,
Hate in a crumb, in the grinding of tram wheels,
In the vin du bistro and the mumbling monologue,
Hate in a harlot's shoe, in the priest's breviary leaves,
In the oil greasing a lathe, and the cobbler's broken awl.
Hate backwards and forwards, in the axles turning and all their echoes,
In the May Day muguet and the iron flowers of November,
Hate in the leaves fallen and the red buds to come,
In the breeze and the frost and the pool, in all the dying and renewing,
Hate climbing the curve of the circle—
Look look how the womb fills—like a moon approaching the full.

(1941)

FRAGMENT IN THE OLD WORLD

Here comes an angry little moon,
A russet bauble in an indifferent sky—
Who wrote "It may be Prester John's balloon",
And who "Theirs not to think but do and die?"
Oh fitful quotes, your strophes ring like the hours,
Begone, and let me get my furrow straight—
Oh quotes that want to glove each circumstance
And lead the poet to your Walpurgis dance,
Be gone.

    Gin we drink from weariness,
    Gin we drink through dreariness,
    Metal-mouth gin, desist—serve us no quotes today.

"Theirs not to think…"
In Lybia, Penang, or the old imperial squence—
But theirs to think and do in Russian snows…..

                                          (1941)

INCARNATIONS

This was the kind of man with his hands on the tiller
Of the little old ship riding wave like a cockle or rocket,
Landing in deep surfs, beaching her sharply, then striding forward
Questing or conqueror over the frozen turf of the north.
He stood on the tops of hills and arid summits
In most extraordinary dawns that started the tremendously long day with a
ritual—
Days longer in ventures than sunlight—
And he would always be planning and thinking
"What is the *best* we can do with these new ones,
For them as well as us…amalgamate this handful of people.."
He was a kind conqueror,
Knowing strength and sanity and the balance of heart, mind and hand.
Finally the day would come to an end. Then he would lie down
In the sheepskins and bearskins and the imported arctic feathers
Of breasted duck and teal, the gold head easy in all this brown and rose
For a little, with a primitive lute-string
Somewhere near, being played for sleep by a heap of hot embers;
All of this very warm in the improvised huts of conquest and in the home
castles.
The shadows were huge then, and the drink strong, very strong;
Was it athelbrose or ale or mead or the berry from the woods..
Whatever, it was made rich and strong, for the transports of strong tired
men.
And in the splendour of blazing logs
Winked a power of great stones, precious ones, with the far-travelled amber
amongst them.
The man sat, thinking and planning still, at the head of the table, silent,
While the new things were brought in from the outlying provinces,
And a message about gold, with news of further tradings,
And pondered while the rest toasted conquest:
"What is the *best* way to use all this?"

And then, after a few centuries,
He is one of two in the interview of two kings—
Look, the same head, eyes that appraise, analysing,
The same build, the same muscling, the poise;
A leader, a poet, one for the arts, but also for statecraft,
One that honours line and the shapes and meanings of flesh—
A meeting of two kings that is going to end the bloody battles;
One of the two is defeated but I do not know which.
It seems as if this man is persuading the other
That even the conqueror does not win;
Life will not halt or dwell on these concepts: *acceptance* of defeat, *triumph*
                                                            of victory.

Such a condition is useless, it does not work.
It does not work for the victor to sit on the vanquished
With armes and tyrannies, rough law-codes, impositions:
"These are the dragon's teeth".

And another time,
Trekking across an American desert, with a flask and a banjo under the
                                                            arm,
Pioneer, buccaneer, emigrant, prospector—
Learning the solitary crag, affiliate with the empty plain;
Night in the juke-box—man's brother; gone by dawn,
On, west. And then a long poem written about the time of sundown
Under a wind-carved pillar, with a vague-à-l'âme—but also with a plan.

(Down the long slant of centuries the metal is always gold,
Old Celtic gold, and the thread blue, that blue and green and grey
Of certain flints—and eyes—that blue as much stone as sea,
Pristine, eternal)

Force out of old northern time: "Contigo pan y cebolla",
The Spanish says it best: "Sufficient with you bread and onion";
More is not asked, all being here—forgetting never:
War within war, man within life, life within struggle—
These must be won.
                                                (1942)

WHOSE DESERT?

Bou Ahmet Ben Sikri Bey foresaw a war;
It came: two hundred thousand into Spain.
Jusef evoked the Riff, baring a scar,
And cursed the *roumis*; then came war again.
Hussein on a car was in it, and at times
Too crazed to pray, then called to Allah: "Heed!
Blow then a stench *accidiæ* from your climes
And raise your devils from the Shott Jerid."
And Maître Tahar, his Tunis now the world,
Mused in a masterly Arabic: "Carthage stood
Where guns now shake and deathly smokes are curled,
Fasces and Swastika—death to their brood—
But after annihilation of these dogs
Whose conquering wing above our Islamic rags?"

London, Nov. 1942.

Notes: The Moors of Spanish Morocco have twice been involved in wars since the beginning of this century against Spain. The war of the Riff which lasted over 20 years and could only be won by Spain due to French aid, waged by the Spanish Monarchist regime against the Arabs, and detested by the soldiers and masses of the Spanish people. Then the war of Fascist Intervention, led by Franco and other rebel generals, which bled Spanish Morocco dry of men and sent scores of thousands of them to their death against the Spanish Republicans in a war execrated by them. The *roumis* are the "foreigners". Hussein is in the fighting against the Germans in Tunisia. *Accidiæ* are certain evil spirits in Arab lore. *The Shott Jerid* is a huge, impressive, now-dry, now-watery salt-marsh. (I have been in it with Norman Douglas.) Maître Tahar is a Tunisian Arab lawyer musing on Darlan and Allied policy and on the future of his country, a protectorate (in rags) of France.

THE RELÈVE AND THE MAQUIS

The mayors put up the Order on the walls:
"Labour, well paid, in Germany today."
Laval found better with these words: *France calls*
All men of France…Each man who goes will free
One prisoner…Duty…Brother…Gratitude…"
Three generations looked at it, and said:
"Grandfather, father, self—we fought the Boches
Each in his youth, then prime—and shall, today.
It's No. The Relève, this changing of the guard,
Is planned for dupes, by Vichy's fear of us;
They want a France unmanned. We shall not go.

And a mean wind blew doubt: "Some of it's true?
No, it is blackmail, lies." And the months crept.
"…Or perhaps one may claim a prisoner? Then if so
Three of us go, if Jean…?" But no. Meanwhile
One million and a quarter prisoners stay in the Reich;
In France comes hunger to sit between nerve and flesh,
Press-gangs for labour, food-cards taken away,
Reprisals on a wife, eight guillotines
Travel the land (till then there had been one),
Shootings and hitting back—But it's always: NO.

In July of '42 the first train comes,
La Relève out of Germany! Blazed in the traitor press,
Staged at Compiegne where Hitler signed and stamped
With fist and foot his Armistice sham as Fascism.
How many men in that train? Three hundred, packed
like a load of curses, sick, and half un-limbed.

He sat in a fireless kitchen head in hands
"From under our feet the ground…and France is done…
Is done? Is *down*. But I live. I'll fight against that."
Just before dawn he unearthed the rabbit gun
And his old revolver blessed by Spain, and went—

To the high lands by the goat track, a wind of decision
Blowing dawn into day. "Wife and life now these two…"
Gun and pistol under knee he sat after the four-hour trek
Till a boy surged calling "Password?"
So the new rhythm began—"We're not a hundred miles from Vichy"
"Nor a hundred months from freedom." Thus into concourse
Of camp—some of sixty, some of sixteen, but mainly those of the young
                                                            twenties:

Ceux du Maquis, francs-tireurs, partisans, guerillas,
"Refractories to law and order" Vichy calls them;
Into the Secret Army the months have made them.

They swore him in: "Enlisted until war's end—
Not to see folks or friends again—Don't count on any pay—
Death if your weapon's lost—Total secrecy, death if not—
Tolerance of each man's views, religious, political—and
Obedience to Maquis discipline in its very hard totality."
Marseille, Lorraine, Angoulême, Lille, Savoie, Franche-Comté,
Paris, Bretagne, Languedoc, Normandie—here is all France.
Loam and letters, student, shepherd, mason, agronomist,
Army-captain, priest, mechanic and a lawyer-poet. Today comes a veteran
Of Spain and of the other two wars each side of that.

As yet there's a gun for every twentieth man—

"Always you hold your hand till the strategy's ripe.
You time your fuse for success. You hold your hand
Till it finds Death's hand responding as an ally.
This is the start. When we have won we shall build
        Not out of *hope*, but out of *strength*,
        Freedom—signed, FRANCE."

Feb. 1944

DORDOGNE

Creysse, Lot, on bank of Dordogne,
Two hundred souls, their oxen, truffle-pigs,
A grey village round a blond castle-keep,
Puffed out with trees, the night-sky pricked with stars
O-brightest-of-all in September-crispest-of-all;
The talk earth-flavoured, the smell of the hot cep in it all
Through the wine and garlic—

Do you remember, Henry
We were there that 1930, and I made you work;
After the day's bucket brought in from the pump
You sat at the piano the oxen had dragged from Martel,
Composed *Henry-Music* and were loved by the people of Creysse:
"A brown man, a beautiful Negro, in a red and blue car..dropped from the sky…
Now look how he plays" they said, and we all drank together at the inn.
We didn't look so much at the world then, that pre-Marchukuo year,
The village was the scene, not death's international roustabouts.
One night I sat on our grey steps and saw her, the old crepuscular,
Bowed over the boiling, the whole boiling, and wrote of her—this :

Steams, but not in any now-dry now-flooding river washes
All the sheet and weave of the region in a slow stew;
Her copper's a day of judgement, compost of noon and night stuff,
Field-sweat, tavern-sweat, love-sweat, death-sweat, all of it,
Heats of maize and tobacco acre, roads and the boisterous market.
Lifting—oh lay brotheress—all these robes smartly, while she grieves
To a little girl attendant of the grease that groans
In crease's prison, of the tears
Old dribble and spent sweat print on the square of
Shirts, of the tortured *strings*, telescoped, corkscrewed
Enfeeblement of *pot-wipers*, wrenched *bib*, *kerchief* invalidate
Its colour-with-age-I-tell-you prismed,
And the plain dust itself in the *apron*!
Shameless this tough green
Woollen that will no down, with its goose-gabble.

Hierarchy—the big ones go underneath,
The ill-thought-of *valence* and the history of a windy night—
Cheek by jowl by *towel sheet*,
Et la *serviette éponge* qui sut se marier;
Mayor's *frill* and drover's *wipe*..
That *summer-blouse* was before her first—

The graillon's in the glory-hole..soot!
Blood's brown braggadocio come to your reckoning..
Auspice! Hog spit on it—vanishing of vanities—
Cunning the red winestain: to ink thou shalt return.

Not a bubble out of the load,
Appointed all, with a quiver of *socks* at copper-brim,
And here's a month's chat slowly, slow-ly...
Old yes-and-no woman
DOWN with the stars into the pot
And UP with the devil—company's company
...Where a pin's none...Sangdieu!

      She sets four stones
Cardwise on her stacked pyramid, and the sparks prick
Fire into charcoal nightlong, and she pats it.....
"Si c'est pas *honte* de ne pas envoyer tout ça plus tôt—
A perishin' shame on them sending me all that at one go."

 Dordogne,
Land of the walnut, chestnut, goose and vine,
(Land of red hearts), land of caves prehistoric.
Chellean, Magdalenian, Musterian, Cro-Magnon man
Left more than a line or two here: the rump of a bison
Limned in ochre or umber, the curve of a feline
Crouched, the span of a taut bow.
Land of red hearts—today the *maquisards* are on the *causse*
In the sparse thyme of winter, raking of the shepherd's hut
A stockade with bombs and rifles, somewhere there above Rocamadour
Somewhere above Marennac, and Fages, the great ruin,
Places like that—
The red heart turned into armed fists against the Boches and Vichy
On the causses, the high stony remote empty hilltops—
Salut, best of peoples and regions; we shall meet again.

 Dordogne,
All day in Lascave's entrail the stalagtite drips to the stalagmite.
 Dordogne
All day all day wives wash against your stones...

O time with dual face, now whole, now facet,
Speed the great battles. *Mort à l'envahisseur*;
And to all traitors, double death.

 (1930, 1943)

Maquisards: Those who have taken to the *maquis*, the wilds; in this case the *causse*—to defy the Nazis' and Vichy's order to go to forced labour in Germany. Today thousands are in the maquis in various parts of France, many of them in the Limousin, the region around much of the Dordogne river. Often they have defeated the armed guards, German and Vichy, sent to bring them in by force. They are organised, helped by the population of whatever region they are in.

(This is the poem for GERMANY in "PASSPORT TO FREEDOM" 7
poems to 7 countries, not yet finished.)

GERMANY

Öd und leer
Eine wüste—
Bavarian dreamer where are you today?
      "In Dachau, Buchenwald—*bin Moorsoldat,*
A soul on a moor where Death and Time are warders.
A soul? With a body foresooth; the body, a ball and chain
Dragged until out by order of the bullet
Or torture in the hideous dawn or the last vesperal flogging.
      Knife, lash and hatchet:
See the scutcheon of the *Herrenvolk.*
      Once this was a human land,
An old grey green river between castled vineyards and legends,
The dappled Rhineland and the smile between the apple-trees,
And Heine's songs—here the heart wandered like a lover—
Aus meinem grossen Schmerzen
Mäch Ich die kleine Lieder,
I know not what we can make of ours,
The cofferdam's full to the brim but leaded with silence.
      This was a place once
Of spirit and intelligent courage;
Now they've turned life into *Ersatz*
In Hackenkreuzland—and where the hammer strikes
It strikes alone to break and not to make…"

And a voice rang over the moor "
"Todt ist kein Ersatzding im Russischen Schnee"
(No, death's no ersatz in the Russian snows.)

"You remember öd und leer? It referred to a sea
Where no sail showed—it is Wagner's *Tristan*—
Came the sail bearing Isolt, and the tune changed
Late, late—too late, for all its joy. So for us, late
Is the sail over the waste of years, the flute plays to very many dead,
Falters, resumes. It will not bring back Erich Mühsam."

Another said:
"While you chattered 'peace in our time' and everything shook because the
                                              base was rotten,
Hugged child whispering 'Can't happen here', keeping your politics warm
on the hob,
And the facts swelled in their ghastly sequence leering back at you in the
                                              chapter called Munich,
We were here with our pickaxes, spades,
In our fog, our fury, our silence;
Here were we—we, the veterans."

A travelling wind blew over the dirty snow
With a clang of battle and a song in it, and a man said:
"That is our Thaelmann Kolonne in the streets of Madrid."

In the sullen northern dusk the shadows come and go,
Look close, each is alive and most are strong;
And the mist turns into sound, the sound into singing :
        "Victory, though not the action—
        I have seen Victory coming but not the action,
        The way, the year it will come."

When the tide bursts free remember this and these,
Saying : *Not conquest of men but victory over war,*
And what makes it, the Hackenkreuz, the Fasces.

London, Dec. 24, 1942.   "Life and Letters Today", June or July 1943

MAN SHIP TANK GUN PLANE

GUNS far away—then last, closest. And ring-wise or splayed out? Like
                                                                    London
Arc, 50 by 30. At night. How uncharted the problem of sound,
Though the middle-ear's filter salutes, comes up at the double to solve it,
Hurt most by a break in the scurry, by the pause that resembles a wound.

No thing is confused; all's in order. Time noted. Last *lares penates*
Pressed finally after long years in small bag on the couch wait the hand,
Ready for "smartly"…"fare onward". So, pacing, sireenly…(O sister,
You turned one, telling the Yanks "'alf a blitz 'alf a mo'" on the Strand)…
Come *mine*, mine-mine…mine, between 10 and 10.1, the all-closest (guns
                                                                    I mean)
And the heart of it nears, yes? It does. It breaks up and the pattern is lost,
Lost, no, but scattered, forked-out now; ah look, the sound cedes it to
                                                                    vision—
Have we storm? We have storm…*peak,* maybe—(keep it patterned
                                                    whatever the cost),

Storm-at-sea…Round this Horn yet…All's relative…Mount, climax, then
                                                    decrescendo…
Peak—only fools wave-count—it's *peak* counts, thrust up through this giant
                                                    tattoo…
Percentage of average…8 million…*but for soldiers in battle, this, always,*
Who say: "If your name's not on it why then it is never for you."

Rage rave in your high loft majestic—for look, now the wild horses have it
Burst loose in the dizzy skies in their crazy mad gallopade,
Rearing-careering—like planes, yes…can hear them—and roaring-
                                                    careening,
Part-sound, part-vision, part-sensed—planes sniped in an air enfilade.

So! Down-come of satellite steels, cascade of the shrapnel olives,
Casual flora of lead bloomed on street, iron spawn from the sky's black
                                                    breast,
Then up-gush of incandescence, and crystalline chandelier
Christmassing down from 12,000 (the purpose amidst the feast).

I told you: sound yields it to vision—Then the guns, flares, glass, crash,
tracers
Condense of a sudden on "*There?*" Do the flames sit in west or east?
More like in the south—no, Soho—somewhere back of the plays and Eros,
(*Superb* is the fireman's skill)…And what now? The whole night's at rest.

I know—you hate these things written—wanting bluebell a-quiver in
heather,
The secular flight of lone heron in lieu of massed iron wing,
Seeking olive at peace in grey stone-land, and glint on wild fur and feather
From sunrise and sunset, and ruins where only the *long*-dead sing.

Bat into seagull, welcome! Delft on its old shelf safely,
With only for trepidations those of the sewing-machine;
Turn fresco of flames into tide-piece, match gull's wing with stone-white on
Downland,
Some time hence scarred turf will renew battle-slough revert to March
green.

Some time hence they will come, I suppose, mood and time to weigh and
consider
What metre best fits what matter…If the Love-Courts were just in their
day…
Man will study old specious disputes, things like "the sex of angels"…
Some, turn to the pink in a flint, and the artisan's osier way.

∧   ∧   ∧

But NOW, no. None of such. All's at war. In front of me sea, and it's
FRANCE;
And beyond that, the past, and it's SPAIN. Death hurls down a comrade's
lyre:
Mid-March it is Alun Lewis, death precedes him with Nordahl Grieg;
The whole face of one dream is SMOKE, and the voice in the next shouts
FIRE

Loud, loud, in the ear. Long, terrible, gaunt the enforcement of waiting—
Does the wind from above blow chill, is there sign to vouchsafe us a date?
Here day after week and month after year, and in vassalled countries,
Man burns: "It is I, one being, but I in my millions, *I wait*,

And…nought?" Nought, nought, and nought, *nothing*—impeccable
                                                        Nothing,
Round as the total circle with zero at full in the midst,
Hinged to invisible vacuum, suspended in seasonless ether,
Greater than unlaned ocean, static, nor "last" nor "first"

In its nature, like Time. Like Time? Ah! but Time is live too, is imperfect,
Subject to change, has springs, and when they are darkly pressed
UP, peoples! haste history; come, dictators and traitors, to trial—
Convulsed are the panoramas, and see, when they fall to rest

Cuts through the dust-cloud THE TRUTH, as spare and white as pure
                                                        bone is.
All must march in appointed order: Man flies across the West,
Man triumphs on in the East; when the South is dynamited
The North skirls down convergent—so must it come at last.

Dèpart à zéro. Our say. The fifth spring. The initial and ultimate
Surge, that the feet have learned and the years stored up—till it come
With its roar and tornado, its science, its vigour, its fury, its lava,
At last, like a mistral-boreal—CHARGE—sure as the African drum.

THEN, YES—to the arts of peace, to their modes and themes and values,
When the armies have battled through, and the dragons' teeth have sprung
Sown wide by the conscript millions exiled in teuton death-land,
And the worker clasps the soldier, and the *Marseillaise* has swung

Freedom into fulfillment. Then yes, to a measure of heart's ease,
In a room at The Rising Sun, with a drink to all races' increase—
The landscape no longer khakied, the man on the rick with the hayfork,
And the tank led out with the horse to furrow—Piers Plowman at peace.

East Chaldon—Dorchester   March, 1944

Notes

The dating of poems in brackets in the text and all the notes that precede or follow individual poems are Nancy Cunard's and have been left as found in the typescript she prepared for publication in 1944.

ADOLESCENCE, l. 25. 'The winter spent at this came Tennyson' is what NC has written, but can hardly be right. 'After the winters spent at this came Tennyson'?

TWO SEQUENCES FROM "PARALLAX". The date 1923 refers to the composition of this particular poem, rather than the book *Parallax*, which was published two years later. Both this and the poems that immediately follow show NC's attempts to absorb the criticisms Ezra Pound had directed against the poem she sent him in 1921. (See Introduction.) Hence the abandonment of iambic pentameter and the use of verse notation similar to that in CATHAY. The influence of Eliot is even more apparent.

LOVE'S ALBA AGAINST TIME, ll. 13-14, 'And as Aragon has it / Aima, ai-ma'. The quotation is from Louis Aragon's 'Poem a crier dans les ruins' (1929), written at a time when he had just about ceased to be NC's lover.

BETWEEN TIME AND ETC. Ernest Dowson (1867-1900), a member of the Rhymers' Club and friend of Lionel Johnson and W. B. Yeats. NC may have come to know his poetry through Edgell Rickword, another one-time lover of NC and an admirer of Dowson's work. Dowson was always 'Having it out with time and love', most famously in 'In Tempore Senectutis' ('when I am old, / And all Love's ancient fire / Be tremulous and cold', and the double quatrain containing the unforgettable 'They are not long, the days of wine and roses').

TELL IT, GLEN. The fifth National Hunger March started from Glasgow in January 1934 and reached London in February. NC's poem is one of a number of writings about this particular march, the best known of which is probably the 'Song of the Hunger Marchers', words by Randall Swingler, music by Alan Bush. For more on this see Andy Croft, *Comrade Heart: A Life of Randall Swingler* (Manchester University Press, 2003) pp 44-5.

AND ALSO FAUSTUS. NC had met Tristan Tzara in Paris in 1924. At that time she was working on a French translation of Marlowe's *Doctor Faustus*, which Tzara planned to stage, although the plan was never realised. Then, early in 1931, he became a signatory in support of her private screening of Dali's *L'Age D'Or* at a Wardour Street Cinema. The 1935 Writer's Congress in Defence of Culture, convened by a committee of French writers including André Gide, Henri Barbusse, Romain Rolland and André Malraux, was held in Paris in June of that year. Among the British writers attending were Aldous Huxley and E. M. Forster, the latter of whom would later record his appreciation of Gide's 'moving speech … about the greatness of Man, who will become greater still when no men suffer from misery and want.' See E. M. Forster, *Two Cheers for Democracy* (London, Arnold, 1951) p 236. Because Forster kept a certain distance from the extreme left in Britain and sent a disclaimer to NC about *Authors take Sides* ('I do not feel that manifestoes by writers carry any weight whatever') he has been largely and quite unjustly written out of the record of what happened on the left during the 1930s and indeed 40s.

EOS. This seems out of sequence if the poems are reckoned in purely chronological order. I assume that NC wished to drop this into the middle of her poems about Spain in order to show that the Spanish war was part of a wider conflict. The reference in stanza 8 to the Anschluss, Hitler's annexation of Austria in Spring 1938, is therefore germane in allowing the reader to understand that the official British policy of non-intervention in Spain has also permitted the tide of Fascism to spread across Europe. In Greek myth Eos is the goddess of the Dawn, the daughter of Hyperion. The dawn the poem envisages is both one of horror and possible deliverance. 'Volubilis' (l. 57) was a Roman settlement constructed on what was probably a Carthaginian city, dating from the 3rd Century BC. It was a central administrative city for this part of Roman Africa, responsible for the production of grain in this fertile region, and exports to Rome. The city also played a key role in relations with the Berber tribes, who the Romans never managed to suppress, and who only appear to have cooperated with the Romans out of mutual interest.

SEQUENCES FROM A LONG EPIC ON S P A I N

'**December 1936, Madrid**:' The Battle for Madrid, which had begun in earnest on November 8 1936, had ended on the 23rd of that month with both sides exhausted. After another two weeks, Franco was forced to give up his plans of taking the city. The International Brigades had played a vital role in defending Madrid from Nationalist forces.

'**December 1937**:' '*They did not pass*—through Toledo Gate'—The Toledo Gate (Puerto de Toledo) marks an important crossroads of Madrid. The route here connects the city with the suburban areas across the Manzanares River.

'**The Exodus from Catalonia—Republican Spain walks into France—Jan-Feb 1939**:'—On 26 January 1939, Barcelona fell to the Nationalist Army. The President, Manuel Anzaña, and his government moved first to Perelada, close to the French border, and, then, as Franco's troops moved ever closer, escaped to France on 5 February. NC wrote several prose accounts for the *Manchester Guardian* which appeared in early February 1939, describing the plight of the Spanish refugees. For examples, see Hugh Ford, ed., *Nancy Cunard: Brave Poet, Indomitable Rebel*, pp. 191-97.

THE LANDS THAT WERE TODAY. Chamberlain declared war on Germany on 3 September 1939. Kay Boyle, an expatriate American writer whom NC met in Paris in 1923 when Boyle was a mere 20 years old, and with whom she remained on friendly terms, visiting her at the end of Cunard's tour of Chile and the West Indies in 1941. For more on Boyle see Frederick J. Hoffman, *The 20's: American Writing in the Post-War Decade* (London: Macmillan, 1962).

PSALM FOR TRINIDAD. This, with its echoes of Vachel Lindsay and Stephen Vincent Benet, may seem a less than tactful exercise, but in fact NC was enthusiastically received in Trinidad. A local newspaper, *The People*, pointed out that her 'famous' anthology, *Negro*, had been banned by the colonial authorities. In addition, she was known to be a 'Negro sympathiser'. Calypsos were written in her honour, including the following:

When talking about outstanding visitors to this Colony,
Who wouldn't be proud and glad to see
A lady who has an open mind and fair
We mean Miss Cunard here to enjoy our tropical atmosphere.

Her works as we know are widely read,
Some of the few we laud, and instead
Of blaming her for writing about the Negro,
Authors should have taken the subject up long ago.

See Chisholm, pp. 260-1.

'I am Butler, Uriah Tubal Buzz Butler of the Oilfields' (l. 13). The Oilfield, or Butler, Riots as they were called, were a water-shed in the political history of Trinidad and Tobago and marked the beginnings of the revolution of the labour movement not in only in Trinidad and Tobago, but in the entire English-speaking Caribbean. Butler (1897-1977) was a key figure in the riots which lasted from 19 June to 7 July 1937, during which time they spread to all categories of workers in the country. Following the riots, Butler was imprisoned from 9 September 1937 to 6 May 1939. With the outbreak of the Second World War in September 1939, Butler was re-arrested under defence regulations and detained for the duration of the conflict.

'I am the poet Cruickshank, my Wordsworthian line...' (l. 43). Alfred M. Cruickshank (1880-1940). His *Poems in All Moods* (Port of Spain: Surprise Print Shop) was published in 1937. Many of the early Trinidad poets were strongly influenced by (and imitative of) English models. See Sander, *The Trinidad Awakening*, pp. 40-41. Reflecting on his time as editor of *The Beacon*, Albert Gomes remarked: 'What I found, in the days of *The Beacon*, was that the verse I received, for the most part, suffered because of the incrustations of a culture not its own, in both form and content. But cultural illegitimacy apart, it also was anachronistic in the sense that Yeats, Pound and Eliot had already written, but Trinidad was still with the English Romantics and their thee's and thou's and overblown gestures'. Albert Gomes, '*The Beacon*', *Kraus Bibliographical Bulletin*, 31 (August, 1977), 158-59 (159).

TO ALFRED CRUICKSHANK. See previous note.

GERMANY. The reference to 'Die Moorsoldaten' ('The Peat Bog Soldiers') is to a well-known song of the socialist and communist political resistance, composed and sung by those imprisoned soon after the Nazis came to power in 1933.

MAN SHIP TANK GUN PLANE

Alun Lewis (l. 43). Alun Lewis (1915-1944), Welsh poet and short-story writer, died on active service in Burma in March 1944.

Nordahl Grieg (l. 43.) Nordhal Grieg (1902-1943), Norwegian lyric poet, dramatist and novelist; a socially committed writer whose resistance to the Germans during the occupation of Norway and whose death in World War II made him a hero of post-war Norway. Grieg died over Berlin on 2 December 1943, whilst acting as a journalist/observer on an Allied bombing raid.

Index of Titles and First Lines